ADVANCE PRAISE

Dr. Helen Holton masterfully blends wisdom with actionable strategies, making this book an invaluable resource for leaders at any stage. Her unwavering commitment to empowering others shines through every page, inspiring readers to lead with purpose, authenticity, vision, and intent. I am delighted and honored to share my heartfelt testimonial for my dearest friend for over forty-five years; her ability to connect deeply with people and her passion for fostering growth is truly exceptional. *Intentional Leadership* is a testament to her remarkable journey and work with transformative impact in the world of leadership-a powerful read for intentional leaders!

— Adrian E. Bracy, MBA, CPA
Author, Executive Leadership Coach
Retired CEO, Greater St. Louis YWCA
Former NFL Executive

The topic of leadership never grows old, particularly in times like these where complex societal issues, racial divides, and threats to democracy test our faith in a brighter tomorrow. This time demands hope, intentionality, and a heart for the human spirit, and Dr. Helen

Holton's book is a remarkably personal and practical guide. It provides a purposeful blueprint to navigate uncertainty every step of the way. Wherever one might be on the leadership spectrum, this book is for you, and women will especially find affirming attributes of their innate strengths as keys to optimizing their effectiveness and impact in a world that needs their light.

— Laura Johnson
Senior Vice President, Chief Acceleration Officer, Social Impact Accelerator
United Way Central Maryland

Dr. Helen Holton's *Intentional Leadership* distills decades of experience, navigating complex community systems into a powerful formula for change. Drawing from her success in education, governance, and non-profits, Holton offers leaders a blueprint to transcend divisive rhetoric and foster genuine progress. Her approach transforms diverse perspectives into strengths, enabling teams to break through entrenched barriers and achieve meaningful societal advancement. For leaders ready to build bridges and drive impactful change, this book is an essential guide to creating alignment and moving forward with purpose and pride.

— Seema Alexander
Founder, Disruptive CEO Advisory
Creator, UNIQUE Method™
Co-organizer, DC Startup Week

Intentional Leadership explores how strengths, values, traditions, and beliefs shape a leader's style. The author, inspired by her father's influence, shares her journey to becoming an intentional leader. With enriching insights from John Maxwell and Barack Obama, this book offers practical wisdom for aspiring leaders. Beautifully intertwining personal stories with powerful leadership principles, Helen Holton highlights the importance of authenticity and purpose in leadership. This is a valuable read for those looking to lead with intention and integrity.

— Sharon M. Weinstein, MS, RN, CRNI-R, FACW, FAAN, CSP
CEO, SMW Group LLC
Partner, Diagnostic Think LLC

As an international healthcare executive who has worked with over 5,500 organizations globally, specifically in leadership development, I wish I had a tool like Dr. Helen's *Intentional Leadership* to reference. She has written the playbook for anyone seeking their passion and vision for transforming their leadership. Her journey has been anything but easy, but her honesty and practical tools, like the pillars of intentional leadership, understanding your strengths and working with a professional coach all add value to the investment you make in your leadership growth and the development of those you lead. Dr. Helen Holton has given us a road map to success that includes passion, pursuit, and purpose.

— Duane Taylor, PhD, Esq, MPP, MCPH
Consultant, International Executive Healthcare

In a world of rapid change and increasing complexity, leaders are seeking greater clarity on their role and how they can be impactful. In this book, Dr. Helen gets to the core of what is required of leaders. Through her vast experience and nuggets of wisdom, one comes away not only inspired but equipped to take our leadership to the next level. In story after story, she pulls us in with her personal experience and deep insight, then applies it to the demands of today. This book is invaluable for those who want to shorten the path to leadership mastery.

— Dr. Irvine Nugent, PCC, CSP
Partner, COPIA Leadership

Dr. Holton's focus on intentional leadership has been transformative in my leadership journey since 2019. Our first meeting was under extraordinary circumstances; our entire school community was unexpectedly relocating just one week prior to students returning. In this challenging situation, Dr. Holton's coaching, questioning, and reflective practice provided my staff with hope and a sense of resilience. Over the past five years, these practices have been the cornerstone of our school's success, leading us to be named one of the 50 Most Improved Schools in the state of Maryland. *Intentional Leadership*, as Dr. Holton practices it, provides a clear roadmap of practices that, if followed, will result in improved productivity, better leadership decisions, and enhanced leadership practices.

— Peter A. Thompson, EdD
Principal, Forest Heights Elementary School
Gallup Certified Strengths Coach
National Association of Elementary School Principals (NAESP)
Certified Principal Mentor

In *Intentional Leadership*, Dr. Helen Holton delivers a masterclass on leading with purpose and clarity. This book is a powerful guide for anyone seeking to elevate their leadership game by being intentional in their actions and decisions. It's a must-read for those who aspire to inspire and drive meaningful change within their organizations and communities. Prepare to be empowered and equipped with the tools to lead with intention and achieve extraordinary results.

— Dr. Willie Jolley
Hall of Fame Speaker, International Best-Selling Author, Award Winning Singer, and Host of the #1 Self-Help/Motivation Show on Sirius XM

As a Black woman serving on the executive team of one of DC's largest city agencies, I found this book to be incredibly inspiring. What struck me most was its format, which skillfully distinguishes among three distinct pillars, allowing for a structured approach to exploration and reflection. This compartmentalization enabled me to delve deeper into each aspect, fostering a profound self-awareness that is crucial for both personal growth and effective leadership. I wholeheartedly recommend this book to leaders at all career levels and emerging leaders aspiring to grow and excel. Its thoughtful approach and actionable insights make it essential reading for anyone committed to personal and professional advancement.

— A. D. Rachel Pierre, MSW, MBA
Administrator, Family Services Administration
Government of the District of Columbia

What I know for sure is that *Intentional Leadership* offers rich nuggets of value-added knowledge for your leadership. The "Intentional Leadership Shift" section has not only driven me as a successful leader but also enriched my personal and professional career and that of my team. I am deeply grateful to you, Dr. Holton, for sharing your gifts and making a tremendous impact with your book. The strategies and tools you have provided are not just for the moment but for a lifetime. Thank you for your guidance and wisdom.

— Annette Fisher, MBA, PMP
Chief of Marketing, Maryland Aviation Administration

INTENTIONAL LEADERSHIP

HOW TO DRIVE LEADERS, VISIONS, AND TEAMS FORWARD

INTENTIONAL LEADERSHIP

HOW TO DRIVE LEADERS, VISIONS, AND TEAMS FORWARD

Dr. Helen Holton, MBA, CPCC, PCC

Press 49
4980 South Alma School Road
Suite 2-493
Chandler, Arizona 85248

Copyright © 2024 by Dr. Helen Holton. All rights reserved.

Published by Press 49, a division of BMH Companies, Chandler, Arizona.

No part of this publication may be reproduced, stored in a retrieval system, or transmitted in any form or by any means, electronic, mechanical, photocopying, recording, scanning, or otherwise without the prior written permission of the Publisher. Requests to the Publisher for permissions should be addressed to the Permissions Department, Press 49, 4980 S. Alma School Road, Ste 2-493, Chandler, AZ 85248, 833.773.7749, or online at www.press49.com/permissions

Limit of Liability/Disclaimer of Warranty: While the publisher and author have used their best efforts in preparing this book, they make no representations or warranties with respect to the accuracy or completeness of the contents of this book and specifically disclaim any implied warranties of merchantability or fitness for a particular purpose. No warranty may be created or extended by sales representatives or written sales materials. The advice contained herein may not be suitable for your situation. Neither the publisher nor the author shall be liable for any loss of profit or any other commercial damages, including but not limited to, special, incidental, consequential, or other damages.

Scripture quotations are taken from the New International Version translation of the bible, copyright ©1973, 1978, 1984, 2011 by Biblica®. All rights reserved.

The views expressed in this publication are those of the author; are the responsibility of the author; and do not necessarily reflect or represent the views of Press 49, its parent company, or its partners.

Volume pricing is available to bulk orders placed by corporations, associations, and others. For bulk order details and for media inquiries, please contact Press 49 at info@press49.com or 833.PRESS49 (833.773.7749).

FIRST EDITION

Library of Congress Control Number: 2024909755

ISBN: 978-1-953315-44-1 (paperback)
ISBN: 978-1-953315-45-8 (eBook)

BUS071000 BUSINESS & ECONOMICS/Leadership

Cover and interior design by Medlar Publishing Solutions Pvt Ltd., India
Back cover photo of Dr. Helen Holton by EYEImagery
Printed in the United States of America

I dedicate this book to God,
the source and strength of my life who sustains and
keeps me, orders my steps, and loves me unconditionally.

And to my mother,
Barbara Marie Goodwin Holton Cuffie,
one of the most resilient persons I know.
I love you to life everyday, more than you know.

This book is also dedicated in memory of
family members who added value to my life.
I am grateful for who they were,
and I miss them immensely.

My maternal grandparents,
Stephen Cornelius and Helen Jefferson Goodwin
My paternal grandparents,
Hiroam Bruce and Lara Hardee Holton
My father, Hiram Holton
My brother, Hiram Holton Jr.

CONTENTS

FOREWORD

In the ecosystem of intentional leadership, there is a difference between good intentions and being intentional. Good intentions have to do with starting out, and being intentional has to do with completion. Having good intentions is initiating, and being intentional is follow-through; having good intentions is dreaming about it, and being intentional is doing something about it!

Dr. Helen Holton's *Intentional Leadership: How to Drive Leaders, Visions, and Teams Forward* is all about being an intentional leader. She challenges the reader to recognize leadership as a series of intentional acts. It's leadership that is not accidental or coincidental. It's leadership that is not a byproduct of good intentions but is the byproduct of discipline, planning, and execution.

I've had the privilege to watch her be a committed and concerned public servant, a leader's leader among elected leaders, a strong community activist, and a preacher of the gospel. Witnessing her transformation was and continues to be a joy!

Dr. Holton weaves her personal leadership journey with wisdom gained through her lived experiences. You will be inspired to step outside your comfort zone to dare the improbable and the impossible. She stands ready as an accomplished executive coach who intertwines human action with divine intention that becomes the gold standard of intentional leadership. Read. Share. Grow.

Bishop Vashti Murphy McKenzie
President and General Secretary
National Council of Churches (NCC)

ACKNOWLEDGMENTS

Adrian Bracy, Catherine "Cathy" Dixon-Kheir, Denise Harris, Denise Simmons-Graves, Diane Hutchins, Duane Taylor, Linmark "Tony" Pearson, Nicole "Nikki" Ross, Terri Parker, and Yvonne Holton, thank you for your thoughts, insights, interest, love, and support for being part of my "A" Team. I love you for who you are in my life. Your open, transparent, and authentic presence in seeing me, standing with me, and believing in me undergird me to bring my best to the world.

I extend my heartfelt gratitude to the following people whose expertise and guidance were instrumental in getting this book to the finish line:

My National Speakers Association DC chapter, with a special shoutout to Sharon Weinstein, Willie Jolley, Karen Snyder, Sylvia Henderson, Irvine Nugent, Omékongo Dibinga, Haley Foster, John Watkis, Tonda Bean, Candy Campbell, Alison Shapiro, Shelley Row, John Edwards, and too many others to name here who give of their time; talents; and treasure of knowledge, wisdom, and experience as speakers, coaches, authors, and more.

To Cathy Fyock, Deborah Peaks Coleman, Melodie Powell Boone, and Lois Creamer, thank you for your passion and gifts as book coaches, authors, and speakers. You are the book writing professionals I reached out to as I stepped into this space of authoring my own solo work. You were my cheerleaders who continued to encourage me to press forward.

To the members of my writing and publishing team, thank you, Bridgett McGowen-Hawkins and Press 49, for your patience, guidance, flexibility, and support. You didn't give up on me, you hung in there, and the world is the better for it. And to Alyssa "Ally" Berthiaume and The Write Place, Right Time, you are the best! I am grateful to your understanding, collaboration, compassion, and challenge to up my game and focus on how best to share my story to add value to leaders everywhere. Words do not adequately capture our journey together. You are an editor extraordinaire! I look forward to the books that are waiting within.

Seema Alexander, the Disruptive CEO, and our work together to deconstruct and bring alternative perspectives to the flow of my Intentional Leadership Process System™ through your U.N.I.Q.U.E. Method™ was pivotal. It pushed me to be laser focused on reframing with greater clarity the process and success achieved by leaders, teams, and organizations with which I've been privileged to work.

Finally, to all the leaders who trust the process and who have joined Dr. Helen Holton and Associates to become part of the movement to develop leaders into intentional leaders, the world needs you now like never before.

INTRODUCTION: INTENTIONAL LEADERSHIP IS A LIFELONG JOURNEY

"The power of intentional leadership lies in the ability to turn a vision into reality through deliberate actions."
—John C. Maxwell, American author, speaker, and pastor

Growing up, I dreamed of being a leader, calling the shots, and being the boss.

Hiram Holton was the first entrepreneur I knew. He was my dad, and I was a daddy's girl and his firstborn. He was the owner and operator of two full-service gas stations and a collection of real estate rental properties. He loved running the show and took on the good with the bad. For a man with a high school education, he did quite well. He made being a business owner look easy, attractive, and desirable. He was the boss. Not that I fully comprehended what that meant then, but if it was good enough for my dad, then it was what I wanted, too.

I never lost sight of that dream. Over the years, I put in the work—education, internships, leadership development programs, coaching, training, false starts, missteps, and failures. Today, I am an entrepreneur, the owner of a boutique business, and I am the boss.

Being the boss entails much more than the average person believes. It's not for everyone. To be successful at it, you have to really want it and be willing to roll up your sleeves to do the work. As an intentional leader, I lead through my strengths, flaws, resilience, imperfections, well-being, humility, and God's grace. I'm living my best life ever with a brighter future still yet to come! What I didn't fully comprehend as a child, I understand today and am actively engaged in working with leaders to drive their visions and teams forward. Every single day. With intention.

This book is about the leadership journey of my life—what I've learned and am compelled to pass on to others. It encompasses some of the ups, downs, flat roads, detours, distractions, and dreams all in pursuit of purpose, passion, and calling. It's not always smooth sailing. Sharing stories that have shaped the growth and development of this unicorn will hopefully motivate and inspire you to look at the trajectory of your leadership and identify the leaders within your team or organization. Maybe it's time to consider what it means to pursue higher levels of success, fulfillment, and joy beyond your comfort zone.

Leadership is shaped primarily by your strengths, values, traditions, and beliefs. This book guides leaders on how to become more intentional about your leadership. We all have gifts and talents that enable us to make valuable contributions in the world. Intentional leaders gravitate toward the responsibility and desire to teach, guide, manage, mentor, train, and coach others to learn, grow, and give back to the world in meaningful ways. It may sound a bit pollyannaish or altruistic, and that's a good thing.

Our world is starved for leaders who care and exercise some level of altruism. Intentional leaders have a genuine concern for the welfare and well-being of people. The COVID-19 pandemic gave the world an opportunity to take a hard look and reset the environment of human engagement in the workplace. Your role as the CEO, senior vice president, executive director, division head, section manager, or some other leadership title charges you with delivering outcomes for a team and/or organization. Or, you may be reading this book as an aspiring leader, someone on the rise to leadership. You, too, are invited on this journey.

The journey to intentional leadership begins with you. Some of us are meant to be leaders, and if you are reading this book, on some level, you believe that about yourself. Your style and sense of leadership is unique to you, as it should be. No two leaders are exactly alike. You, as a leader, are influenced by leaders who have invested in you. They have impacted your leadership by investing in you with their time, talent, energy, wisdom, feedback, networks, resources, and more.

Throughout this book, you will learn about the foundational pillars of the Intentional Leadership Process System™, the signature program of how my company, Dr. Helen Holton and Associates, works with leaders to drive visions and teams forward.

Having worked with over 500 leaders, teams, and organizations as a coach, trainer, consultant, and speaker, using customized content from my Intentional Leadership Process System™ allows my team and me to delve deeper into the practices of achieving intentional leadership.

INTENTIONAL LEADERSHIP SHIFT

Becoming intentional about leadership and showing up as an intentional leader require a shift. An intentional leadership shift is beyond a simple change you implement to be different. It is a transformational and purposeful shift from who you were to who you are becoming, fueled by your intent to lead better—the kind of leadership shift people notice without you making reference to your shift.

An intentional leadership shift is something you take on like a dog with a bone. The analogy comes from watching my beloved puppy, Max, for years shift his behavior and perspective when given a bone—not an ordinary bone but one to improve his oral healthcare, like Greenies. Those little, green-shaped bones captivated 100 percent of his attention until each one was totally consumed. His determination and intent to eat that dental bone to completion taught me about making shifts to achieve the fulfillment of goals. Commitment, consistency, and focused attention taught me essential elements that make intentional completion possible.

The push and grind of working to be a better leader can be like a roller coaster ride, up then down, and back around again for the same ride. When you're in constant motion to do something without intention or specificity, you can get caught in the trap of procrastination, avoidance, and excuses over things you say are important to you. Talk is cheap, and everybody's doing it.

It is time to do a new thing—with intention. If you are looking for a breakthrough to take your leadership to the next level, you must be willing to step out of your comfort zone. Be bold. Be brave. Be daring enough to confront yourself honestly and take some risks into the unknown, even if it frightens you. Your breakthrough could very well be on the other side of your fear.

The things that never move from the back burner of your life to the forefront begs the question, "How important are they to you, really?" Sometimes they don't move because you're not ready to explore them as viable options. It might mean you're distracted with other necessary aspects of living—like keeping your head above water—that can dampen or delay your dreams and your intentions. Don't allow your delays to be denials of your destiny. Patience is truly a virtue.

When your focus is to pay bills, have fun, eliminate debt, save money, and become a responsible adult, you can easily squeeze out your big picture plans that you cannot see down the road...yet. To have more freedom, charting your own course can be confusing and exhausting without a plan, purpose, and intention. Giving serious consideration about what it will take to transition from where you are to where you want to be is the beginning of purposefully aligning your thoughts, words, and actions with your intention. That is when you know you are ready for an intentional leadership shift.

Being good at making excuses to justify being stuck in the status quo can keep you holding on to your comfort zone. How do I know? Because holding on to my comfort zone was my excuse for far too long. It's not that I didn't want to move forward—I just didn't move the way I envisioned and dreamed I would.

Choosing intentionality and deliberate action to shift is a lifelong journey. Just because you figure out one thing doesn't mean you won't need to figure out something else later. Intentional leadership is not a static posture; it's a dynamic and ever-evolving part of life.

THE BIRTH OF THIS BOOK AND WRITING YOUR OWN STORY

My friend, John Maxwell, *The New York Times* bestselling author, speaker, coach, and leader recognized as the number one leader in business by the American Management Association, gave me a book. Okay. It wasn't just me. He gave everyone in the room that day—hundreds of us—the same book.

In March 2022, I attended my first in-person International Maxwell Conference since becoming a certified member of the John Maxwell Team several years earlier. At the end of his training at the conference, he handed each of us a book and shared what a wonderful gift we had just received. It had an interesting title, *The Greatest Story Ever Told*. I remember thinking, "What a thoughtful gift." As someone who loves books, I felt valued to receive it. It was the accelerant that led to the completion of this book.

I had proclaimed to friends and family in 2017 that I was going to write a book to share my story. Finally, seven years later, the fruit of intentional leadership was released. John's gift of a blank canvas was the driving force to finish this book you're reading now. His gift, which pushed me to complete this book, is truly the manifestation of one of my own intentional leadership shifts.

Upon opening the book, at the time I first received it, was an endearing message from John C. Maxwell. As I turned the page to peruse the table of contents, there was none. In fact, there were no words on any of the pages. It was an empty book of lined pages. A journal. A blank canvas. A creative and innovative way to invite each of us to share our own unique story. The foreword to the book was a handwritten message from John that started out, "Dear Friend, The Greatest Story Ever Told can only be written by you." The book was actually a companion journal to accompany his book, *Intentional Living*.

John's opening message was simple and was followed by a few reflective and introspective questions, befitting the master coach that he is. The first question convinced me to move beyond my false starts and fears. I became intentional about sharing lessons learned from personal experiences that could be of value to others—others like you with a desire to be more intentional in your life and leadership. Placing the book in a prominent place was the accountability that kept me committed to action.

That journal with its blank pages and a few questions to ponder became the canvas to create, prompt, and serve as a constant reminder of the unfulfilled commitment to my purpose, passion, and calling. It took some time to push through procrastination's hold and fear's grip on me to step up and into living life consciously as an intentional leader on the other side of "Yes!" Barack Obama became the forty-fourth president of the United States running on a theme of "Yes We Can." And, together, we can become more intentional in our leadership.

Sometimes it's the questions that pique your curiosity the most that send you on a journey you did not know you were going to take. And, when you become intentional about the journey, it produces transformational results for you, the lives of others you touch, and those to whom you add value.

INTENTIONAL LEADERSHIP ON PURPOSE— AN INVITATION

As a leader, you impact and influence the lives of other people, directly and indirectly. Getting clear on your why and the difference your contributions as a leader can make matter. However, it matters most when you're anchored as an intentional leader because that's when you're leading at your best.

As a leader, the unique talents and gifts you have contribute to making the world better. When you share your life lessons learned to support or enhance the leadership development and growth of others, this is a good thing. It's a way of paying it forward in recognition of the leaders whose shoulders you stand on today. Imagine how much more impact your leadership can have when it's executed with intention.

Your unique contributions as a leader can be made only by you. No one else can make them like you. If you haven't invested in optimizing your leadership with intention, what are you waiting for? This book was written to help leaders just like you become more intentional about your leadership.

The words and spirited stories shared between these pages are from my heart, head, and lived experience, and I've included some from other leaders living their truths. They represent lessons learned. They speak to the strengths, values, beliefs, vulnerabilities, upsets, and resilience that helped to make this book possible.

It is my belief that this book will move you forward in living a more fulfilled, imperfect, perfect life as a leader that no one else can live the way you can. Your gifts, talents, and contributions as a leader are needed now more than ever. This is your personal invitation to join the journey forward to make the world a better place as an intentional leader. Let's get to it!

CHAPTER 1

THROUGH THE LENS
OF A BLACK WOMAN

"Nothing is impossible. The word itself says 'I'm possible.'"

—Audrey Hepburn, British actress and humanitarian

The complexities of who I am that influences the writing of my leadership journey lives at the intersections of race, gender, political power, and privilege. I was born Black and female in America in the early days of the civil rights movement. It's the lens through which I live, breathe, and have my being as a child of God.

The identity and experiences of my life are shaped by the complex interplay of these four intersectional factors. They have shaped challenges and advantages faced throughout my life. I share this information to highlight the need for leaders to understand the unique and overlapping forms of discrimination, inequality, and injustices encountered due to the convergence of these and multiple other identity factors. Acknowledging the intersections of identity is crucial for promoting inclusivity and social justice, as it recognizes the complexity of human experiences and helps to address systemic leadership challenges from a more comprehensive perspective.

The context of my existence is shaped by more than 400 years of bondage, oppression, discrimination, and exclusion. Systemic racism, conscious and unconscious bias, white privilege, and greed have perpetuated and sustained an inequitable societal construct targeted and placed upon people in America.

Twenty-one years of public service as an elected official and eight years as the executive director of a national nonprofit organization afforded me the opportunity to experience America from coast to coast. The subtle and not-so-subtle cultural differences that co-exist in communities throughout the United States can be as different as night and day. As a woman in leadership, the experiences widened the aperture of my lens and reshaped my perspective on what it takes to lead well.

On April 12, 2015, a twenty-five-year-old Black male in Baltimore City was arrested and taken into police custody. While in the back of a police transport vehicle, he sustained injuries that landed him in a coma by the time he reached the hospital. Seven days later, that young man, Freddie Carlos Gray Jr., took his last breath in the emergency room of the University of Maryland Medical Center. He was still in the custody of the Baltimore City Police Department. How did this happen?

This was the first time in my role as a public leader where the question, "What does it mean to be Black in America?" hit home for me in a very personal and communal way. It means that the value placed upon your life as a person of color in America carries a false narrative of "less than," "not good enough," and "dispensable." And, since 2015, it hasn't gotten much better. If the truth be told, it's worse.

The day Freddie Gray died changed my life as a leader in a profound way. As a senior member of the Baltimore City Council, it was an awkward and embarrassing awakening. It happened on my watch. It challenged my leadership. I asked myself, "How was I complicit in this loss of life?" Incidents like this don't always lead to physical deaths, but they all contribute to psychological deaths of people and communities.

Had I done all I could have done to dismantle biases—conscious and unconscious—that made situations like this common, daily events? Today, I can unequivocally say "No. I should have done more." The duty, responsibility, and accountability to my community as a Black female leader are nothing to take lightly. It was an unconscious, ugly, and painful truth that looked me in the face. And it demanded a response.

The events that took place following Freddie Gray's funeral are still fresh in my memory like it was yesterday. It was an overcast afternoon, and after spending hours inside of Shiloh Baptist Church for a politically charged and emotional farewell, it was refreshing to stand outdoors and breathe fresh air. The climate outside was anything but calm. There was a storm brewing, an uneasiness you could feel in the atmosphere—literally and metaphorically.

Freddie Gray's death unleashed a wave of pent-up frustration and disgust over the realities of what it means to be Black in America. Rioting, looting, and property destruction persisted for days. This defining moment was a call to do more and be more committed with focused intention. Nothing this dramatic, tragic, and on public display for the world to see had occurred here since the riots after the death of Dr. Martin Luther King Jr.

The tragic and senseless deaths of Black people in our communities reveal the ugly, naked truth of systemic racism, unconscious bias, and white privilege displayed in some of the most depraved acts of unnecessary and unwarranted violence and hatred. We see it all around us every day, and in many ways, we have become blind and numb to the injustice it represents, going through the motions of life with benign neglect.

The COVID-19 pandemic was the most significant global paradigm shift in a hundred years. In a very indiscriminate way, it showed us that race, ethnicity, class, sexual orientation, and whatever other classifications of separation we can muster didn't matter to the coronavirus. It's an equal opportunity virus for which no one gets a pass. We are all susceptible to it. It's an equalizer of sorts. It was a moment of an undeniable truth.

We must believe we deserve better before we can begin to actualize what better looks like. It requires focused intention, commitment, and discipline. It demands a collective and collaborative effort. The Montgomery bus boycott of 1955 lasted 381 days—thirteen consecutive months. It launched a major national push towards fairness and equal treatment you may know as the civil rights movement. Many of the freedoms enjoyed by you and me that might be taken for granted were paid for with the price of many lives.

Like Fannie Lou Hamer, an American voting and women's rights activist, I chose to do something about it. I was sick and tired of being sick and tired, and this was an opportunity to put up or shut up. The interconnectedness of competing and conflicting systems such as racism, sexism, classism, ageism, and others complicate the challenge. It cries out for intentional leadership. I committed my life to build bridges; break down barriers; and work to cultivate more diverse, inclusive, and engaged strengths-based leaders, teams, organizations, and communities.

To be Black in America means you belong to a resilient group of people who have faced discrimination, hatred, injustices, and other atrocities since landing on the shores of North America. And we're still here; we've not been annihilated. We continue to press forward toward better because giving up is not an option.

There is good news, and it begins with a change in your attitude and a shift in your mindset. Moving from awareness to action begins with waking up to the conditions that keep you down and get in the way of your greatness. Be intentional about everything you do. Untapped knowledge lives within each of us. Where there is hope, there is always opportunity for better. This is what drives me to do this work every day and to tell the story.

REFLECTION QUESTIONS AND NOTES

When working with people from cultures different from your own, how do you experience and express your frustration, conflict, or confusion?

____

____

____

____

Make a list of specific cultural differences you notice.

____

____

____

____

Identify three actions you are willing to take today to understand and lessen the tension you feel or have felt.

____

____

____

CHAPTER 2

WHAT'S HOLDING LEADERS BACK?

"The biggest room in the world is the room for improvement."
—Helmut Schmidt, chancellor of West Germany

Effective leadership is a delicate dance, and even the most seasoned leaders face a myriad of challenges that can impact their ability to lead successfully. We will address four prominent pain points or challenges leaders often encounter that interfere with their leadership. To delve into how these challenges manifest in your leadership is the beginning of understanding what may be roadblocks to your success.

As you read through these symptoms, make note of the ones you feel are present within your leadership, team, or organization. Noting these can help you identify the opportunities for improvement.

INEFFECTIVE COMMUNICATION

Clear communication is the lifeblood of any successful and intentional leader, team, or organization. When leaders struggle with ineffective communication, it creates a ripple effect that can be felt throughout the entire workforce of the organization and sometimes beyond.

For example, one time, I was working with a leadership team where the leader desired to recalibrate their team to be on one accord. The overarching goal was to work more collaboratively, focused on a common agenda. I opened the training, asking a volunteer to share the vision of the organization. What I got as a response was a deafening silence.

This was an eye-opening revelation in real time. Following an uncomfortable pause for the team, someone chimed in that it was printed in the front foyer of the building where everyone enters. This made an unpleasant truth even more glaring. This was an indicator, an example of ineffective communication.

Using this awareness to establish a perspective for our work together aided in moving the team further along with improving internal and external communications. The work began with gaining clarity on their vision beyond catchy words and slogans. They were able to see the disconnects that were destroying their ability to work well as a team. Being intentional about co-creating a new vision with buy-in from the team gave them the leverage they needed to achieve goals and work better together as a connected and unified team.

Challenges of ineffective communication manifest in various ways:

- **Misunderstandings:** A lack of clarity can lead to confusion among team members, resulting in tasks being performed incorrectly or not at all.
- **Low morale:** When communication breaks down, team members often feel neglected and uninformed. When the people you lead do not feel seen or heard, it leads to a decrease in overall morale. Without intervention, you can be facing a downward spiral from which it is not easy to quickly rebound. Low morale is often indicative of burnout, "quiet quitting," and higher turnover.
- **Missed opportunities:** Important information might not reach the right people at the right time, causing missed opportunities for innovation, improvements, or investment in people for greater growth.

RESISTANCE TO CHANGE

In today's fast-paced, hectic, and mixed-up world, change is inevitable. The COVID-19 global pandemic is over. However, the VUCA (volatility, uncertainties, complexities, and ambiguities) presence we continue to face daily is on steroids. If that sounds a little harsh, it is. Not every leader embraces change with open arms. As a leader, how often do you find yourself clinging to resistance in the face of change? Recognizing the signs of resistance is crucial. Change cannot begin without it.

Public education took a beating in the area of burnout during the pandemic. It continues to lead in cases of burnout among teachers, administrators, and support staff. I began work in this sector before the pandemic, and resistance to change was pretty high then, especially around the new school year and reaching full staffing levels.

Processes for engagement and communication, especially around hiring practices, experienced significant changes as a result of the pandemic. Returning to pre-pandemic practices without considering better and more efficient processes is an example of resistance to change. Principals overwhelmed by resignations, extended medical leave, and "quiet quitting" have left too many leaders in public education struggling to find a way out.

Here are a few ways resistance to change shows up:

- **Lack of engagement:** People on your team may disengage from their work or express reluctance to participate in new initiatives in addition to those in progress. These are signs of burnout, stress, and active detachment or "quiet quitting," leading to total withdrawal. This can happen consciously and unconsciously.
- **Increased turnover:** Are you a leader with a strong aversion to change? Your resistance can lead to talented team members seeking opportunities elsewhere, resulting in higher turnover rates for you and the organization.
- **Stagnation:** An organization resistant to change risks becoming stagnant and unable to adapt to evolving market trends; technological advancements; and generational shifts in values, beliefs, and traditions.

CONFLICT MANAGEMENT

Conflict is a natural part of life in any workplace, but when left unmanaged, it can escalate and become a significant obstacle to success. Identifying signs of conflict mismanagement is critical.

While working to confront tensions between the top two leaders in a nonprofit organization, the number one and number two were steeped in miscommunications that led to breakdowns in trust and cooperation with increased tensions felt throughout the leadership team and spilling into the organization. The tension was felt in our coaching sessions, and it was clear that productivity was impaired.

What begins as a difference of opinion can sometimes be the precursor to bigger issues that require management of differences for the overall good of the organization as a whole. It is like a snowball rolling down a hill. Once it gains momentum, it takes much more energy to repair and manage to get back on track, if possible. Conflict management can be like a bull in a china shop.

Here are additional ways that conflict management might reveal its presence:

♦ **Tension among team members:** Unresolved conflict can lead to tension and animosity among team members, negatively impacting cooperation, congeniality, and collaboration.

- **Decreased productivity:** Conflicts not managed well can divert energy and attention away from tasks, leading to a decline in overall productivity. Engagement among team members and throughout the organization is adversely impaired.

- **High turnover in leadership:** Persistent conflicts may lead to leaders burning out or choosing to leave their roles, contributing to leadership turnover. This impacts the organization from top to bottom, which is often a bigger gap to fill than turnover among the non-leadership staff. The longer it persists, the more strain it puts on everyone.

BALANCING RESPONSIBILITIES

Leaders often wear multiple hats, juggling various tasks and responsibilities. When leaders struggle to find balance, it can have widespread consequences. Living in the overload is self-defeating and results in the following:

- **Burnout:** Overwhelmed leaders may experience burnout, which leads to fatigue, decreased productivity, and potential health issues. Health challenges can be physical, emotional, and mental that show up independently and simultaneously.

- **Neglect of important tasks:** Critical responsibilities may become casualties of neglect as you struggle to effectively prioritize. Ignoring them does not make them go away.

They become feeders of frustration that often lead to or exacerbate burnout.

◆ **Team disengagement:** An imbalanced leader can inadvertently create a work environment where team members feel unsupported, undervalued, and out of balance. It is a trickle-down process that, if left unattended, can do as much damage as an ignored leaking faucet that requires a major investment to repair the damage done.

Living in the overload during the COVID-19 pandemic dramatically transformed the expectations of leaders in many industries, sectors, and professions. Working with leaders and teams produced a sharp spike in the challenges of balancing responsibilities. Clients sharing comments that reflected their frustrations, resignations, premature retirements, acknowledgments of difficulties in coping from day to day, and finding balance was disturbing. A few leaders shared concerns about their own mental health instability with feelings of despair with no way out.

By no means are these four areas—ineffective communication, resistance to change, conflict management, and balancing responsibilities—meant to be an exhaustive list of challenges that keep leaders from optimizing their talents, skills, and strengths. The goal of this discussion about challenges leaders face is to help you expand your thinking about the challenges or pain points that interfere with and disrupt your leadership. It's a way for you to begin to identify specific areas in your leadership that could benefit from a shift toward becoming a more intentional leader. I offer this shortlist for you to begin to pinpoint areas that may be challenging you right now.

Throughout the book, I uncover some of the data and research gathered, including interviews with leaders over the past twenty-five years or more that have influenced this book. Work with clients, collaboration with colleagues, and input from peers learned and leveraged have all been factored into this distinctive body of work. The results of my findings are discussed throughout this book along with suggestions on how to address some of these challenges.

REFLECTION QUESTIONS AND NOTES

In what areas in your leadership do you feel stuck? Afraid to take risks? Unsure of yourself?

____

____

____

____

What three pain points challenge your leadership most? Which one will you address first? Why?

____

____

____

____

How will you address your most pressing pain point? How will it impact your leadership?

____

____

____

____

CHAPTER 3

DEFINING INTENTIONAL LEADERSHIP

"Leading with intention requires the courage to make tough decisions and the wisdom to stay true to your values."
—Tony Dungy, former National Football League player and coach

To lead with intention means you approach your leadership roles and responsibilities with a clear sense of purpose, focus, and mindfulness. It involves making conscious and deliberate choices in how you lead and the impact you want to have on people, teams, organizations, communities, and beyond. Intentional leadership calls for a commitment to leadership development, ethical principles, professional growth, a moral compass, and the well-being of those you lead.

Leaders who lead with intention inspire trust, create positive impact, and contribute to the success and growth of the people, teams, and organizations they lead. Throughout this book you will learn about the foundational pillars of my Intentional Leadership Process System™, the signature program my colleagues and I use in our work to drive leaders, visions, and teams forward.

LETTING GO AND BECOMING AN INTENTIONAL LEADER

What does it take for you to become an intentional leader? A willingness to let go—to let go of your excuses, judgments, fears, selfishness, ego, and all the other ways of being that have you showing up as less than who you are at your best. It means letting go of the stuff that interferes with the best possible outcomes you can achieve as a leader.

In the introduction, I mentioned how becoming an intentional leader requires a shift—a transformational shift, which is a more significant and sustainable style of leadership. It requires you to leave your comfort zone and open space for something more. That more is found in your pursuit of intentional leadership. No one can or will lead exactly like you; however, your leadership style will influence the people you lead. Make your leadership intentional, for in it lies your legacy; the choice is yours.

Poet, teacher, speaker, and life coach Safire Rose wrote "She Let Go" in 2003; it's a poem that speaks to your inner resolve to clear away any and everything that could conceivably interfere with your intention to lead well. Letting go can mean different things to different people. I choose to see "letting go" as something we shed from our current circumstance.

The intent is to allow yourself to let go of your "no's" and live fully with the intention of "Yes, I can, and yes, I will." Here's what I mean.

Letting go of my excuses, judgments, and fears of failing allowed me to focus and be intentional about transforming my lifestyle to improve my health. Losing forty pounds and reaching lifetime status in Weight Watchers (WW) was not about dieting. It was about sustainable lifestyle transformation. Success opened an opportunity for leadership as a WW meeting leader. In that role, working to support and guide others to champion their goals with weight loss as the driver would not have been possible if I was not able to let go of self-sabotaging beliefs.

FAILING FORWARD IS GROWTH, NOT WEAKNESS

Intentional leaders become successful by taking risks and reaching into the unknown with a grounded belief that you can succeed and be intentional about doing so. Holding on to a position, title, or size of a paycheck is not necessarily a measure of sustainable success or intentional leadership. They can all trap you into an illusion of happiness and successful leadership.

Living life afraid with a lack of self-confidence (in your ability to move beyond your comfort zone) minimizes you. Subconsciously holding onto—maybe even clinging to—a false sense of safety and security often comes at the expense of your dreams. F.E.A.R.—or false evidence appearing real—can be a stronghold that keeps you from living and leading intentionally. It can hold you hostage beyond rational reasoning. The interesting thing about the fear of failure is that it can distort the truth about what's possible for your life.

Servant leaders experience disappointments and disasters not necessarily as defeats but as growth moments marked with grace and gratitude. Dumb decisions—and we all make them—serve to keep us humble. We may choose not to acknowledge them, at least not out loud, but we know when we make them more often than not.

Learning to accept loss, failure, and defeat as powerful growth lessons can propel you forward. They are opportunities for you to think, be, and do more. These are not easy things to acknowledge, let alone accept. It requires you to have an honest conversation with yourself.

When you can acknowledge them to yourself without beating yourself up is when your growth moments become the most powerful for you. Intentional leaders use these experiences to "fail forward." Disappointments, disasters, and dumb decisions can make you stronger and more aware of not thinking more highly of yourself than you should.

Each of these unpleasant realities work to teach us the value of humility. Leading with humility can help you become a more successful leader and a servant leader. Too often, we assume that leaders who openly display their humility are weak leaders. This is far from the truth. Leaders who lead others as servant leaders are some of the most influential leaders around.

CHOOSING TO COMMIT TO CONQUER

To illustrate the points about growth, failure, disappointment, and humility, let me tell you a story. I went to college to become an accountant, graduated, got a good job in public accounting, and decided to pursue the highest achievement of the profession—to become a certified public accountant, a CPA. Those three letters after your name open doors of opportunity.

Becoming a CPA was one of the things that drew me to the profession in addition to my natural knack for numbers. The experience was one of the most challenging in my early adult life. I learned about failing in a very painful and powerful way. My failure and disappointment were humbling and caused self-doubt about my ability to achieve the most coveted status of my career choice.

The CPA exam was a rigorous two and a half days—nineteen and a half hours—when I sat for it. It was a grueling exam given only twice a year. And then it took three months to get your results. The vivid memory on that August afternoon, holding the envelope with exam results in hand, is one never forgotten. I was excited and anxious and told myself, "Calm down. You've got this," which calmed my nerves enough to open the envelope.

Opening that envelope was my first experience of failure with professional implications. I did not pass the exam the first time around, the second, or third either. It was a profound learning and humiliating experience at the same time.

There are times in your life when you must be committed to win it—to go all in. Commitment like intention is a conscious choice you make to achieve what's important to you. It's where you learn to fail forward for the win. It isn't easy, it doesn't happen overnight, but it is doable. Commitment combined with resilience will equip you to achieve more.

Motivation hadn't been enough the first time. It required something more. Being coached through a CPA review course taught me the importance of commitment and how to fail forward. I tried other unsuccessful methods before finding the right fit for me was through coaching. Borra CPA Review course was my path to success. The founder and our instructor, Jim Borra, was a phenomenal instructor and coach.

A highly educated man with more professional credentials than any other person I knew, he was formally known as Dr. James C. Borra, Esq. CPA, CMA, CIA, JD, and MBA. More important than his credentials were his ways of engagement with us, his students. He was funny, personable, impactful, and influential. He held us accountable to our why—how to become CPAs. The time spent with our CPA review coach taught me how to make a commitment "F.U.N."

Now, understand this—there's nothing fun about failure, however, when you make your commitment F.U.N.—focused, unyielding, and non-negotiable—you become unstoppable. I passed the CPA exam by adjusting my perspective and making the commitment F.U.N.

T.D. Jakes says, "You cannot conquer what you are not committed to." I am Helen Holton, CPA because I embraced commitment and made it F.U.N.—focused, unyielding, and non-negotiable—to intentionally achieve the goal.

I share this story to demonstrate what it looks like to take a roundabout approach to achieve something important to you without having the wherewithal or confidence to know what you are capable of completing. It took several years to become a CPA with starts and stops along the way. Not knowing what I know now added to the disappointment, frustration, and doubt in my ability to achieve it. It was something inside me that would not quit. If you are reading this book, I know that the same thing lives within you.

This book was a start-stop endeavor until I looked failing in the face and remembered what it took to achieve my CPA designation. What was needed to complete this book was an intentional focus with an unyielding spirit and a non-negotiable attitude. I committed to making it F.U.N. and incorporated the power of intention, taking a winning formula for how to succeed and making it better by learning to lead with intention!

Repeated failure and defeat through that experience was a humiliating period of life. Riding the roller coaster of feeling confident and secure to insecure and fearful almost robbed me of my destiny. Learning to accept loss as a growth opportunity instead of defeat became the challenge that moved the needle forward for me. How you successfully conquer your greatest challenges often teaches you transferable skills you can use in other areas of your leadership and your life.

INTENTIONAL LEADERS ARE SERVANT LEADERS

Ultimately, intentional leadership is not about you, but it's about being the best version of yourself so you may better serve others. Intentional leaders are some of the most effective leaders because their focus is directed outside of or away from themselves. They seek to equip and empower others as a win-win for everyone involved.

To live your life as a leader who serves others brings benefits to you—joy and fulfillment that exceed your expectations. That is one of your measures of success, and being intentional is the driving force. One of the highest forms of effective, sustainable, and intentional leadership is putting others first—also referred to as servant leadership.

When you become intentional about being a leader, others become the beneficiary of your knowledge and experience. It shows up as an outward manifestation of the power of your attitude and a shift of your intention to lead better. To command your ability as the driver to equip, empower, and elevate the success and transformation of others' success is energizing, affirming, and teachable to others. The people you lead deserve nothing less.

In the words of Zig Ziglar, "Attitude, not aptitude, determines altitude." This truth is available to anyone willing to reach for something more—something more authentic, transparent, and self-seeking beyond yourself. Aptitude is important, but your attitude is more powerful. It is the real driver of your altitude. The choice is yours.

THE STATE VS. INNATE INTENTIONAL LEADERSHIP

Innate intentional leadership is not a smooth or pretty process. Awareness of your strengths has the potential of instinctively showing up without your conscious awareness of what they are. It pulls on your values, beliefs, and cultural traditions. Sometimes it shows up as in-the-moment, on-the-job training that you are internally driven to pursue as a leader.

One of the most thought-provoking questions I've pondered through life is "Are leaders born or made?" I believe it is a combination of both nature and nurture. Some of your talents and strengths are innate, meaning you are born with them; they come naturally to you. Leadership is also nurtured or developed in different ways like formal education, professional training, and life experiences.

There are times when you can hold a title and not be an effective leader in your role. Holding the title is not the same as being the leader; they are not interchangeable. The good news is you can learn to grow and develop into the intentional leader you have the potential and opportunity to become.

The most effective leaders are servant leaders. Serving others above self and striving towards the greater good hold places of high value and integrity for intentional leaders. You lead with intention out of duty, responsibility, and a combination of nature and nurture even when you do not recognize it as intentional leadership.

That experience rang true for me personally when it was displayed in real time as one of my most intrusive, unexpected, and life-altering experiences that dragged on for almost three years. The choices, decisions, and outcomes were reflective of what leading through your strengths looks like when you are not aware of your strengths—when you cannot name them; know what they are; and let alone, know how best to leverage them.

In January 2009, hit with an unexpected public accusation of wrongdoing, my life was thrown into an uncontrollable tailspin from the start. Getting indicted by the Maryland state prosecutor with felony charges was a living nightmare. But that didn't matter to the masses of people who saw, read, and heard the news. True to public opinion, the conviction mentality before a trial made the shock of it all very surreal. Have you ever had your name and reputation falsely called into question? It doesn't feel good, especially when you know it's not true.

As a senior leader of the Baltimore City Council, this disrupted the reality of the body politic; all of us were impacted to varying degrees. From city council colleagues to the mayor's office, career government staffers, citizens of Baltimore City, and the public at large—all were privy to the public opinion of the media as it unfolded, a real time personal crisis on the public stage. Calmness and confidence were nowhere to be found. The tipping point of this living nightmare unfolded while I was out of town attending the Maryland Association of Counties winter conference in Cambridge, Maryland.

While sitting with a couple of colleagues in the conference hotel lounge, debriefing our activities of the day, we were interrupted by the local news on television. Our attention quickly shifted when we heard those words of interruption, "breaking news." On the screen, in living color, was the city council president commenting on actions taken in response to the announced indictment.

It was a surreal and sobering moment of unexpected news that shocked us all as we heard it. To be removed from your leadership role as chair of a major standing committee without so much as a courtesy call or notice was unfathomable. It was like having someone stab you in the back and slap you in the face at the same time. Trust, respect, and integrity were called into question in a moment's notice…publicly. It impacted both the giver and the receiver.

Wow! What a way to find out you've been stripped of your leadership responsibility based on unproven allegations. No forewarning. No attempt made to deliver the news directly or privately before a public press conference with the media. Shocked and blind-sided by the actions taken based purely on allegations was a blow that hit hard. Thank goodness for the presence and support of colleagues with me to help mitigate the situation and maintain a public façade of strength under pressure. On the inside, a total meltdown was in process.

The person you believe yourself to be in your gut, intuitively and instinctively, makes a difference. It reflects how you show up as a leader. Knowing who you really are at your best is essential to your ability to fight your battles and win, especially the unexpected ones. Will you win every battle? No. But when you know yourself through your strengths, you'll win far more than not.

As a leader, knowing who you are through your strengths, through what you do best, is important. It's like your compass that keeps you headed north toward the peak of the mountain top. Leaders lead others. Think about the people you follow. What makes you follow them? What qualities, attributes, habits, and strengths do you notice and admire about them? Are you in tune with how you influence others, particularly the people you lead?

The experience of this devastating attack on my character, reputation, and integrity happened without knowing what my dominant strengths were. However, I'd already invested in resilience (which we'll talk about in a later chapter), and it helped to keep me grounded when life felt like every step was on quicksand. It was a stretch and a blessing at the same time. Deeper learning while going through emotional trauma gave me a better understanding of the power of resilience. It made me stronger. It helped me endure.

The process began months before the indictment was issued in 2009, and the indictment process went on through the courts for a little more than three years until it reached its finality in the spring of 2012. It was a challenging, grueling, and ugly season like none other—truly a unique experience. It tested my nerves, my resolve, my faith, and a host of other emotions to boot.

Have you ever heard the saying "fair-weather" friends? When you can truthfully recognize and acknowledge the fair-weather friends in your life, those who are there only during the good times, you are building your resilience. Once you've had that conscious awakening about fair-weather friends, you should be able to spot them sooner than later when you find yourself in a difficult or challenging situation.

When indicted, I didn't pick up on who were my fair-weather friends and acquaintances right away. The shock of everything happening so quickly caught me off guard. However, once I'd rebounded enough to better assess the situation, they quickly became identifiable in my consciousness. This allowed for a swift shift and pivot to keep moving forward.

Imagine showing up to work every day and having to put on your game face to move past building guards at the front door as well as colleagues, staff, and visitors throughout the building. All the while, you're wondering from whence your strength, courage, and grit are coming to get you from the parking garage to your office. You do it because you take responsibility as a leader. It's less about what you feel on the surface and more of what your gut is telling you is the right thing to do.

Something as simple as walking into city hall to go to work on behalf of the people shifted from a daily ritual to an almost insurmountable challenge. Have you ever experienced a time in life when you had to put on your game face to keep from falling apart? I had to put on my poker face walking in and out of public spaces to present a model of what it looks like to be a strong, solid, and secure leader in the world—to be an intentional leader. Different from imposter syndrome, it was an intentional act of leaning into strengths, activating resilience, and being intention about my leadership. When you get sucker punched as a leader in the public, you still have to show up and lead.

Safeguard your character, reputation, and integrity, for they take time to build and can be knocked down in the blink of an eye. Technology and social media have become a much more powerful tool that can make or break your public and private image. Be ever on your guard and know the trusted people in your life who really know who you are beyond the media. This was a saving grace. When you have trusted friends and colleagues, wise counsel, a belief in yourself—even your ever-evolving self—you've got a stronger start toward success through your struggle.

The fight wasn't easy. There were casualties along the way and hundreds of thousands of dollars in legal fees. But there was also a strong faith and God's grace that led the way to an incredibly successful resolve. A precedent was set to clarify the role and what was indictable for a local elected official in Maryland so as to prevent future frivolous challenges from being brought in what seemed more like an exercise in creating personal notoriety than seeking justice. I saw first-hand the injustices that exist in our judicial system and society that continue to be a struggle and offense to all people who fight for justice.

When all was said and done, I was vindicated by the circuit court, the court of special appeals, and the court of appeals levels of the Maryland judiciary. I won the re-election to my final term in office by a wide margin! It was the nastiest and most vicious campaign I'd ever endured. There were relationships that were damaged, and some were severed forever. A very personal learning was the power of forgiveness.

Forgiveness frees you to live stronger and more resiliently. Forgiveness is more liberating to the giver than the receiver, the person who wronged you. They don't always know that they've hurt you. This is something you must determine and own if you believe you've been wronged. It's about your own liberation—freeing yourself. Forgiveness does not mean restoration of whatever was. It means you're free to live and be open to make new and different choices—wiser choices. This is your opportunity to learn and grow from what hurt you so badly.

In retrospect, I realized my actions during that time often reflected intentional leadership through my strengths. Who you are is who you are. The more you know about who you are at your best can help mitigate or lessen missteps or missed opportunities to lead with intention. Had I known the power of my top strengths (Belief®, Input®, Positivity®, and Strategic®), going through this experience would have been a far less stressful and more manageable experience.

I was driven by instinct and an intention to serve to the best of my ability and with allegiance in my role as a leader of thousands. Faith and resilience were conscious ways of being that supported the journey through the land of the unknown. Intentional leadership is not a fluke. Innate intentional leadership is often not recognized as such until you have an awareness of who you are through your strengths.

Knowing what I know now, what got me through was innate intentional leadership. Leaning into strengths I could not consciously identify then are the ones that allow me to thrive today. Making that connection happens consciously for me today. Your intentionality about your leadership will elevate you as a leader like nothing else.

As a leader, make time to understand who you are at your best through your strengths. Leaders with an awareness of their strengths excel in their leadership, especially when they develop them and use them with intention. We are going to delve deeper into the three pillars of intentional leadership that are game changers for your leadership. Leveraging your strengths is best achieved when you know what they are.

REFLECTION QUESTIONS AND NOTES

How will you make your next big commitment F.U.N. (focused, unyielding, and non-negotiable) to achieve success? What actions will it take?

When you identify fair-weather people in your life, how do you deal with them?

What role does forgiving others hold in your leadership?

CHAPTER 4

THE THREE PILLARS OF INTENTIONAL LEADERSHIP

"A cord of three strands is not quickly broken."
—Ecclesiastes 4:12

Sometimes your awakening can be precipitated by bizarre, unforeseen life events so out of the ordinary that they shake you up to realize your moment to start living with intention is right now. On Friday, March 13, 2020, the president of the United States declared the Coronavirus Disease 2019 (COVID-19) was a pandemic. This was the awakening that led to a shift—an intentional shift in life and, more importantly, in leadership.

COVID-19 had reached a magnitude of severity to warrant an emergency declaration for all states, tribes, territories, and the District of Columbia to adhere to national public health and safety measures to confront what had been deemed a global pandemic. The world was thrown into a tizzy, and life in America (and throughout much of the world) was altered like never before.

Living in Baltimore City and working in Washington, DC presented a challenge with the news. Before fully comprehending what that meant six days later, Thursday, March 19, the mayor of Baltimore, Bernard C. "Jack" Young, declared a shutdown for the city. As a mass transit commuter, taking the MARC train was more practical and economical than driving into DC every day. On Friday morning, March 20, the vivid memory of driving to my office to pack a few files and supplies into my car to transition to a temporary work environment was bizarre. The drive home in compliance with the shutdown was surreal.

It sent my mind into a tailspin of the unknown. The awakening in the disruption of reality led to a new level of trust and reliance on God like never before. It was mind-boggling after the first couple of months that we were truly living in a present state of unknowingness. What seemed temporary was longer than the average person could fathom. No one had lived through a global disease of this magnitude in more than a hundred years. It was a wake-up call for us all. The discovery taking place posed all kinds of questions. One of the most compelling questions that arose in conversations with people was "What do I really want for my life?"

Living life full-out is when you consciously commit to going all-in to live an intentional life. The answer to the question is not just a superficial, off-the-cuff response but one that is backed by deep, introspective thought. It was in multiple common conversations with friends and colleagues wondering about what tomorrow might bring as infection rates and death tolls continued to rapidly rise. Clearly, it was so much bigger than us as individuals. It was about our collective oneness as the community of our humanness. It became very clear that this was a clarion call—a moment to stop and think about what mattered most in your life.

On March 11, 2023, the World Health Organization declared the global pandemic was "officially" over. Conversations, actions, and new ways of being are becoming more frequently prefaced by two different realities: pre-pandemic and post-pandemic life. It's like a seismic culture shift. Our post-pandemic world continues to grapple and adjust to this quantum disruption of difference. The dust has not settled yet—and maybe it never will—and life goes on.

Life is a work-in-progress in a continuous spiral of unpredictable evolution. And it always has been. None of us can avoid it. My purpose, passion, and calling came into alignment during the pandemic. It resulted in a major transition that elevated my sideline venture to the main event of life and livelihood.

The most authentic leaders are those who embody what it means to live in service to others—to live as a servant leader. This is one of the highest callings of intentional leaders. It's what shapes the influence of your leadership and the legacy you leave behind. It doesn't happen automatically. There is a process. It takes time to transform your leadership to be more intentional. Simply put, it requires you to think, be, and do differently. It's like the age-old saying, "If you keep doing what you've always done, you'll keep getting what you've always gotten." That is not progress; it is not the path that leads to intentional leadership.

The best starting place is you. It begins with a serious, soul-searching inquiry of what is your unique purpose to add value to the world. At this stage, you make time to reflect, research, and wrestle with yourself over why this and not that. You begin to consider the rewards, risks, and requirements to move forward into the unknown about you and the world. This is the deliberateness that you apply to explore what it will take for you to move into a space of being intentional about who you are as a leader.

STRENGTHS, RESILIENCE, WELL-BEING, AND PUBLIC EDUCATION

Entry into the world of public education, K-12 in particular, began for me during the pandemic. I grew up believing that being a teacher in public education was traditionally thought of as a sought-after pursuit or calling. Being in a family of educators taught me a lot about the value of a good education. K-12 education is the gateway to the future and introduces youth to the potential of who they can become as adults.

As in any other industry, sector, or profession, it's leaders who drive the success of their teams and organizations. Education is no different in that respect. Leadership is leadership. I learned this firsthand when given the opportunity to work with and engage leaders and teams in K-12 public education. This opportunity continues as a rich body of work and an extremely challenging profession today.

The integration of the three pillars of my Intentional Leadership Process System™ was first recognized while working with schools in the Prince George's County Public Schools district (PGCPS). PGCPS was in search of a solution to turnaround forty of their lowest-performing schools in the district. They chose to invest in a strengths-based approach to improve the workplace culture and talent development for the selected schools.

Through a public request for proposals process, PGCPS was seeking a vendor to provide full staff training and executive coaching for principals. Gallup Inc. was awarded the contract to work with the county with one requirement, and that was to comply with Maryland's Minority Business Enterprise (MBE) subcontractor goals. This was a legislative measure to increase inclusive participation of minority, women, small, and disadvantaged businesses in the state of Maryland.

When Gallup searched Maryland's database of eligible subcontractors, there was only one Gallup-Certified Strengths Coach who was also a Maryland certified MBE, small business enterprise, and disadvantaged business enterprise, and that was Helen Holton, founder and CEO of Dr. Helen Holton and Associates. To become a subcontractor to Gallup was an opportunity of a lifetime. It was a winning combination of leveraging strengths, reliance on resilience, and focused intention.

My first engagement as a subcontractor to Gallup was with the full staff of Forest Heights Elementary School (FHES). I arrived extra early for a meet and greet with the principal, the school's CEO and leader. Dr. Peter Thompson, a tenured career educator and administrator with a passion for his profession, immediately shared a connection.

We launched our work together during the 2019–20 school year with a formal half-day full staff training. We began by unpacking the Gallup CliftonStrengths® assessment results that everyone received and how to understand and invest in their opportunity for transformation. We mapped out our course of action to take place over the first year of this multi-year opportunity. We began the process with a known disruption we knew we'd have to work around.

The workaround for the known disruption was taking place at the school on the day of our first all staff training. They were in the final stages of packing to move for a temporary relocation of the school community of students and staff. The relocation was unavoidable due to major repairs and maintenance needed throughout the entire building. Their temporary location to co-exist with another school was the beginning of our work together around strengths, culture, and resilience.

Midway through our first school year together, the world was blindsided by the COVID-19 global pandemic that interrupted public education like never before. It was like lightning striking twice for FHES. It threw the world a curve ball, and public education took an even harder hit than most other sectors.

FHES survived the relocation from their school building and has since returned. We worked through the COVID-19 pandemic, adapting to virtual online learning for students and staff while confronting challenges no one ever saw coming. FHES has continued to face change; however, they've learned how to lean into their strengths and resilience to keep them going strong. They moved from struggling to surviving to thriving and garnered some top academic honors of achievement in the state of Maryland.

Working with Principal Thompson, his leadership team, and staff continues to be an incredible journey of success led by strengths awareness, undergirded with building their reservoir of resilience that's sustained by an investment in well-being. It didn't begin that way, however, FHES is all of that today and then some.

I share this story because it's a beautiful example of how the three pillars of the Intentional Leadership Process System™, strengths, resilience, and well-being, work together to support the trajectory of your success, personally and professionally. To witness the transformation of a very good leader develop into an excellent, intentional leader is the social proof of the effectiveness of my Intentional Leadership Process System™. The leadership team became solidly grounded as a cohesive team and more creative in their work during the pandemic. They continue to thrive as an intentional leadership team.

Dr. Pete embraced and leveraged his strengths. He took advantage of available courses and training through the workplace culture and talent development opportunities. He absorbed the power of executive coaching and intentional leadership. It kept him focused and moving forward through crisis after crisis after crisis while continuing to soar!

THE BIRTH OF THE INTENTIONAL LEADERSHIP PROCESS SYSTEM™

After years of coaching leaders on how to better lead and serve their teams and organizations, I took a step back to look at what I was doing that made a difference in their leadership success. Working with Seema Alexander, business advisor and founder of Disruptive CEO Advisory, I was able to clearly direct the passion, drive, and purpose of my work to serve leaders better with greater impact on the outcomes they seek to achieve.

The result of our work together is the signature system offered by my business, the Intentional Leadership Process System™. It is anchored in three interrelated pillars that are synergistically aligned to help you become an intentional leader. The process is designed to equip and empower you, as a leader, to lead with excellence and optimize outcomes on multiple levels.

We are about to delve into the three pillars of intentional leadership. Through research, study, and becoming an active practitioner working with leaders through the implementation and integration of these three pillars proved to be the sweet spot for sustainable success. The interconnected relationship among your strengths—awareness, resilience capacity, and well-being—have proven to accelerate and optimize successful leadership outcomes, using my Intentional Leadership Process System™.

The multi-faceted process we use in the Intentional Leadership Process System™ to support the optimization of your best self as a leader is structured to help you do some of the following:

1) learn to leverage your strengths while managing the navigation of your weaknesses;
2) build your reservoir of resilience; and
3) integrate holistic well-being into your daily life.

Together, these three pillars form a solid interdependent anchor to equip and empower you to be a more effective, influential, impactful, and intentional leader.

Each of these working together keeps you moving forward. They can each stand alone and function independently; however, together, they become a unified superpower. Then, you really begin to understand the value of their interdependence to generate optimal results for your leadership and your life. We will explore each of these elements throughout the book as separate components and the additive effect when they work in tandem with each other.

The three pillars of the program are anchored to effectively support each other interdependently. Some of the key characteristics of intentional leadership that are significant to the process are listed below. More about how to use them to shift your leadership from ordinary to intentional comes a little later in the book.

- Awareness and Assessment of Strengths
  - As a leader and coach focused on understanding you through your gifts and talents, in my practice,

we use verified and reliable assessment tools to give you an independent assessment of your talents that hold your greatest potential to success. This is ground zero, the launching pad for you and me to move forward.

- Clarity of Purpose and Vision
  - Long ago, I learned that when you are not clear on where you want to go and why that's important to you makes a big difference in the outcomes you achieve. This becomes your compass to move ahead with some sense of direction and intention.
- Proactive Communication
  - Your command and effectiveness as a communicator are essential to your ability to engage with the people you lead and/or with whom you collaborate to efficiently and successfully get things done.
- Strategic Thinking
  - As a leader, when you can think strategically for the longer term and develop strategies that align with your personal style of leadership, it is powerful. Your context for where you want to go supports your clarity of purpose and vision.
- Conflict Management
  - Managing conflict is a natural part of leadership in any workplace. When left unmanaged, conflict can easily escalate and become a significant obstacle to your success. Identifying signs of conflict mismanagement earlier than later is crucial to your leadership.

* Lifelong Learning
    * Nothing stays the same other than death. Many ascribe to death and taxes. But as a CPA, I can tell you from knowledge and experience that taxes constantly change. The point is that continuous learning helps you to effectively stay on top of your leadership.
* Accountability
    * Who, beyond yourself, holds you accountable to get things done? Having had hundreds of coaching sessions with leaders has proven that self-accountability is overrated. Having a coach as an accountability partner improves your efficiency in getting things done to completion and with higher satisfaction.
* Self-Care and Work-Life Balance
    * All work and no play make a leader less effective than you can be any way you choose to look at it. Our bodies are designed to operate most efficiently with boundaries that adhere to some level of work-life balance. It will shift throughout your life, and being aware of the subtlety of change helps to reduce stress.

The list of characteristics identified above is not an exhaustive list but is a beginning of how to move you toward becoming an intentional leader. The Intentional Leadership Process System™ is customized to fit what you and your team may need. It is a starting point to build upon over time. This journey is a marathon, not a sprint. It is so much more than a quick fix; it is a lifetime commitment that keeps you evolving as a focused intentional leader.

REFLECTION QUESTIONS AND NOTES

In what situations do you feel most connected to your **strengths? Make a** list of three situations that stand out most **for you, then deter**mine how you can use those strengths more.

____

____

____

____

How have you grown stronger and more resilient as a result **of overcoming ob**stacles in your life?

____

____

____

____

How do you balance your personal and professional life? **What adjustmen**ts can you make to enhance your overall **well-being?**

____

____

____

____

STRENGTHS AWARENESS

"Knowing your strengths and weaknesses is one of the most powerful things you can do. It allows you to delegate tasks to others, focus on your strengths, and compensate for your weaknesses."

—Richard Branson, British business magnate

I want to share a powerful message from Don Clifton, the chief architect of the CliftonStrengths® assessment, formerly known as StrengthsFinder®. It was his last email to his son, Jim Clifton, before he transitioned from this life. It simply and eloquently sums up the importance of you as a leader having an awareness of who you are through your most dominant talents/strengths. This is one of the three pillars of intentional leadership. Understanding who you are by how you most naturally think, feel, and behave is the beginning of your strengths awareness.

DAD'S LAST EMAIL TO ME ON STRENGTHS-BASED LEADERSHIP (UNEDITED)[1]

Another notion about leaders is that each one needs to know his or her strengths as a carpenter knows the tools in his box or as a physician knows the instruments she has available, and a carpenter does not hammer with a saw. So leaders have different tools (strengths) in their armamentarium, but the better she knows how to use them the more effective she is as a leader. It is not so much what strengths they possess as leaders—it is knowing accurately what a person has as strengths. (A leader may also need to know her weaknesses, so she can manage them.) This means a leader needs to know what his tools are and exactly when to use each of them.

This explains why nobody comes up with a list of characteristics that describe all leaders. One leader may lead because he has a strength in relating; another may lead because he has a signature strength in competing, or concep-tualizing, or courage, or responsibility. What leaders have in common is that each really knows her strengths, has developed her strengths, and can call on the right strength at the right time.

—Don Clifton, 1924–2003

Don Clifton was an intentional servant leader who left the world with a gift that keeps on giving. This is not the only assessment in the marketplace to help you know yourself through the best of who you are. However, it is one of the most comprehensive and accurate instruments that adds value and insight to you and your development and growth as a leader. It's a solid tool grounded in decades of research, study, reliability, and validity.

WHAT ARE STRENGTHS?— A PRIMER

"Knowing your strengths and weaknesses—and knowing
what you don't know—is critical to real leadership."

—Sheryl Sandberg, American technology executive,
philanthropist, and writer

According to Gallup, the definition of a Strength® is "the ability to deliver consistent, nearly perfect performance in a specific task."[1] As an avid assessment-taker since the 1980s, the intrigue of learning about oneeself through a series of statements, questions, and choices one makes continues to fascinate and facilitate self-learning.

In November 2015, along with fellow board members of the National Foundation for Women Legislators, I took the Gallup CliftonStrengths® assessment as a team-building exercise. It changed my life significantly. It is the bellwether by which I assess the validity of other assessments, and I have taken plenty of assessments upon which to compare with confidence.

The journey into Strengths® was amazing and eerie at the same time. The results were different than any I had ever received before, and they were spot-on. Imagine finding a key that opened a door into more of who you really are at your core. It is a game-changer that continues to have a positive and informative impact on who you are and your ability to lean into it for life to keep going and growing. What is the sustainable outcome? Lifelong learning, continual strengths development, professional growth, leadership legacy, and so much more. The value is priceless!

How I know myself today through my strengths and investing in them has made me a better person and a more intentional leader. When you are better in-tuned to the truest parts of who you are at your best and how to apply them, it's life-altering. It is this awareness and understanding that drives success for you. This helps shape the direction of upward movement for you and the people you lead towards intentionally achieving more success in all areas of leadership and life.

My Top 5 CliftonStrengths® Signature Themes and a brief description of them are as follows:

1. Connectedness®—a bridge builder between people and groups; helps others to relate and rely on each other; finds meaning in the unpredictability of life and provides a sense of stability in volatility; someone who connects the dots while giving others perspective, guidance, and hope woven out of the past, present, and future.

2. Achiever®—has a strong inner drive to get things done fueled by a deep source of intensity, energy, and power to accomplish tasks that lead to goal fulfillment; often shows up as the pacesetter who defines productivity levels for the team, department, or organization you lead.

3. Maximizer®—average is not good enough; excellence is the measure by which they determine success; focused on quality; a natural preference to work with and for the best; strives to create strengths in teams by empowering others to do what they naturally do best; has an ability to set new standards of success through strengths alignment.

4. Input®—collectors of information—facts, words, books, and quotes; gatherers of tangibles like photographs, butterflies, sports memorabilia; strong sense of curiosity and resourcefulness leads them to provide relevant and tangible help to others from their vast collection of stored knowledge and artifacts.

5. Belief®—possess strong and enduring core values that provide clarity, conviction, and stability to support unwavering foundational principles that have the potential to raise the ethical standards of the people, teams they lead and leaders they serve.

This was the first introduction to my most dominant talents. It quickly became the springboard for wanting to know more. The results revealed an awareness that was different than most other assessments I'd taken. It was more directly aligned with the me I most intimately know myself to be along with challenges and opportunities for growth and improvement.

It marked the beginning of my journey into strengths and positive psychology and continues to grow and evolve.

Your strengths will open you up to what is possible for your life through a path of opportunities empowered by you that feel right for you—who you are through the awareness and development of your talents into strengths. When you add a willingness to be vulnerable enough to step boldly into leaning into your strengths, the results are an amazing revelation. Having witnessed the repeated transformation of leaders who reach and often exceed their own expectations using their strengths is an awesome experience.

As of June 2023, more than 34 million people had taken the CliftonStrengths® assessment, and it continues to be improved and refined to help you know yourself better through your strengths and how to use them to engage deeper for greater success and fulfillment in life. It is one of the most accessible and informative tools for human development today.

Gallup continues to refine and improve the CliftonStrengths® assessments. In October 2018, Gallup released the revised and reconfigured CliftonStrengths® 34 report, and in January 2024, they revamped the Top 5 assessment results. It is actions such as these that continue to reflect the reliability and validity of Gallup's multiple assessments. With each refinement of the results, the primary focus continues to reside with your Top 5. These are the ones that capture the quintessential you through the best of who you are!

Leadership and from whom you learn are significant. I believe this is more relevant today than it's ever been.

The proliferation of technology, social media, and artificial intelligence (AI) is overwhelming today. The ability to discern truth from fiction; human processing versus AI; and deepening engagement with the people you lead, follow, and with whom you collaborate is daunting. It also gives rise to the importance of knowing and understanding the power of your talents, what it takes for them to become strengths, and how they work together.

In the fall of 2018, a chance meeting allowed me to test these assertions when I had the opportunity to engage in a one-on-one conversation to explore some of the methodology that keeps CliftonStrengths® evolving and remaining relevant in strengths development. I was attending a week-long Gallup train-the-trainer certification course at their world headquarters in Washington, DC when I had the pleasure of meeting Jim Clifton, the chairman and CEO of Gallup and son of Donald O. Clifton, PhD, the developer of CliftonStrengths®.

The traffic in the DC/Maryland/Northern Virginia area, known as the DMV, can be brutal on any given day of the week. Living in Baltimore and traveling by car to DC can take anywhere from fifty minutes to countless hours depending upon any number of conditions between Baltimore and the nation's capital. I chose to take the commuter train from Baltimore to Washington and eliminate the unpredictable volatility of traffic, and this proved to be a smart choice in more ways than one. Arriving more than forty-five minutes earlier than the course's official start time afforded me the pleasant surprise to meet Jim Clifton and have that memorable one-on-one conversation with him about CliftonStrengths®.

This serendipitous moment was priceless. To speak with Jim Clifton about an assessment that changed the course of my life was epic—a great start to the training to learn from a trusted leader and to learn more about how to use this instrument to evoke transformation for others as a Gallup-Certified Coach on the way to becoming a Gallup-Certified Trainer.

Listening to him share what he learned about himself and using his strengths was worth the early arrival. It was an unexpected bonus. The richness of our conversation and the takeaways from a leader I admired from afar were special.

As a firm believer that there are no coincidences in life, that everything happens for a reason and a purpose, and that we don't always understand what the reason may be at the moment, this was not an accident. I continue to invest in the language of strengths. Looking back over life, I am able to see how the presence of my strengths showed up long before I knew what they were (like in the indictment story I shared earlier).

I learned a lot from Jim that morning and am grateful for the work of his father. In 2002, the American Psychological Association gave Don Clifton a lifetime achievement award, calling him 'the father of strengths-based psychology and the grandfather of positive psychology.'[2]

Awareness of your strengths is the beginning of aligning your abilities and capabilities with your purpose and passion. It's so much more than taking an assessment and glossing over your results before they end up on a shelf, collecting dust. It is an active and personalized roadmap into who you are at your best. What influences the subtle nuances that make you even more unique are your life experiences.

Every experience you have in life helps to equip and prepare you to be more than just a leader. They are the ingredients that feed and shape your life as a human being and fuel your leadership journey forward in becoming an intentional leader. The good and bad of your life have contributed to this truth.

When you identify or recognize the alignment of your purpose, passion, and calling as part of the discovery of your own greatness, it's an awakening. It is an awareness that resonates deep within you, beneath the surface. No one can tell you what that is. Think of it as an awakening of your strengths and how they add value to you in leadership and in life.

REFLECTION QUESTIONS AND NOTES

How do you recognize and know the strengths you possess?

____

____

____

How do you use them to guide and support your success?

____

____

____

What are the most significant steps you have taken to **identify your talents** and strengths?

____

____

____

How will you use them to be a more intentional as a leader **going forward?**

____

____

____

CHAPTER 6

DEVELOPING YOUR STRENGTHS

*"I had no idea that being your authentic self could make me as rich
as I've become. If I had, I'd have done it a lot earlier."*

—Oprah Winfrey, American talk show host, television producer,
actress, author, and media proprietor

Learning about who you are by multiple means and perspectives is an ongoing opportunity always available to you. There are multiple ways for you to embrace, engage, experience, and learn about your specific strengths—articles, books, coaching, formal training, podcasts, and more. Understanding who you are through your strengths helps you, as a leader, build and invest in your leadership development, professional growth, and the lives of the people you lead.

There is a total of thirty-four talent themes/strengths identified by Gallup CliftonStrengths®. Each theme is the culmination of multiple personality traits that are similar in nature and scope. There is not one that is any better than the next. You can successfully accomplish any given task through any one of the thirty-four talent themes or strengths. More on the CliftonStrengths® assessment in a few more pages.

Knowing who you are through your Strengths® is a big deal. As you invest and learn about how they show up for you, the more in-tuned you become to the truest part of who you are and how you most naturally think, feel, and behave. It is who you are at your best. This is the beginning of understanding what intrinsically drives success for you by nature and nurture. It helps shape, guide, and direct your upward movement towards achieving more success in all areas of your life.

REFLECTIONS AND FEEDBACK FROM THE WORLD AROUND YOU

You are the best judge to assess the value gained by knowing yourself better. No person is an island, and the worth of who you are is often reflected by the people with whom you engage and surround yourself. Family, friends, co-workers, and colleagues all help you gauge your value. How others respond to you is an indicator of who you are and what you add or take away from them.

Constructive feedback from others is an opportunity to check yourself against your own sense of who you believe yourself to be. It can be powerful, productive, and sometimes painful in your pursuit to live in your purpose. The contributions you make in conversations, meetings, team projects, or on the world stage are all measurable—but not always by numbers and metrics. Sometimes they're best measured through the shared stories and testimonials of people whose lives you've impacted. These are the ones that I value the most.

What's the purpose of getting input in the form of feedback? How does it factor into your why? The value of what others have received from your expertise can reveal ways you've never envisioned the impact of what you pour out to help them develop, grow, and enhance their own lives. Feedback is also a way for you to see you outside of yourself. The benefit to you is an added dimension of awareness to reflect on the value you bring when you pour into others out of your wealth of knowledge, skills, and expertise.

When you know and affirm who you are as yourself—at your best and worst—it is essential to your own becoming in the world. Connecting with your best self through your strengths positions you to understand how to tap into your greatest potential for success. This is the best way for you to make a unique and indelible impression that only you can make toward our world becoming a better place for us all.

How well do you really know yourself? Think back to a time in life when you realized you didn't know yourself as well as you thought. What was that like? Life can happen in a way that exposes you to what you don't know and can cause real pain points to surface. In a crisis, feelings of fear, frustration, and a sense of loss are valid, and the better you know who you are, the better prepared you are to confront head-on whatever comes at you.

By May 2020, while still teleworking during the pandemic, it became clear that we were in an unprecedented crisis. The interruption the world faced had quickly become an alarming truth of the clear and present danger. Most people were consumed with fear, confusion, and panic. As cancellations, closures, and restrictions increased, the frustrations of our "abnormal life" were mounting by the day. Very quickly, nothing was as it used to be. The infringement was real. The media, colleagues, family, and friends engulfed life with a heightened sense of anxiety, trepidation, and fear. And rightly so—isn't that what the unknown often brings? This unknowingness was over the top for many people.

Faced with a combination of work interruptions and personal life disruption, all happening at the same time, proved to be a bit much. What might have caused a major meltdown in the past was different this time. I found myself in a conscious awareness of how I would maneuver circumstances beyond my control with a calm presence to keep moving forward. The atmosphere around me was chaotic and confusing at times, and I still had a job to do with work to perform. Where was it coming from? What made the difference? It was my strengths at work.

This realization caused an "aha" moment. Amid a rapidly growing global crisis, my strengths were consistently present to me and at work in real time but not like before. This time was quite different in many respects from other past life-altering challenges faced. In retrospect, then, I didn't know myself as well as I thought. The awareness of my strengths and how to harness them in a crisis was missing. When you don't know what you don't know, it doesn't help you grow, especially when you're unaware that something is missing.

SPOTTING BLIND SPOTS

Behaviors that reflect a blind spot of your strengths can create unintended responses from the people who experience you in the overload. Your enthusiasm or focused concentration when fully entrenched in the execution of a dominant talent or strength might cause you to unintentionally repel others. They may avoid you or tune you out because you are over the top and confusing them.

As someone high in Achiever®, I am mindful of my drive to get things done and check them off my to-do list. It is important to recognize when it may exceed the expectations of those working with or for me. I have learned to recognize that when I reach that place, using improved communication and deeper engagement with the people around me helps. The value of having an awareness of your strengths in action is also knowing how they show up in different emotional states...like instances of blind spots, moments of overload, and those times when you need to leverage your strengths with other talents.

If you know team members can feel overwhelmed when you delegate duties, giving them a heads up in advance is an act of you exercising intentional leadership. By being attentive and focused on their behavior in light of you knowing yourself allows you to be forward thinking if and when overload occurs. Your sensitivity and awareness of your own strengths and the resulting workload or deadlines you delegate to team members is a growth moment for you both to better understand each other and grow together. That's a way for you to deepen the engagement with transparency and authenticity.

Having an open-door policy for your subordinates to discuss their growth experiences and vet challenges is a strengths development move. As a high Achiever©, I've learned how to recognize when I'm showing up in overload or with a blind spot. I have found it is best to encourage conversations earlier than later when you recognize your strengths behaving in excess. This is a position that gets in the way of success. Nip it in the bud before it becomes too much for everyone involved—directly and indirectly.

This is a practice I share with colleagues and team members at the onset of our work together. It is good to occasionally remind yourself and others when you are deep in the mix of driving your vision and team forward. Your blind spots and overload of your strengths can alienate you from the people around you like your team and the purpose that brings you to work together.

A blind spot is not to be considered a bad thing; it's a life thing. It can happen to any one of us. Knowing your strengths, their power and edge, the good, and the not-so-good, helps you to be a better leader when you're aware of your blind spots and how to effectively address them.

WHAT DO YOU DO WITH WEAKNESSES?

"Anything that gets in the way of your success" is how Gallup defines a weakness.[1] I love this simple explanation because it makes sense and carries with it a bounty of truth and opportunity for in-depth reflection and consideration. For example, among the thirty-four talent themes of the Gallup CliftonStrengths® assessment, Discipline® appears as number thirty-two in my theme sequence results. In other words, it's nowhere near a top strength of mine. According to Gallup, "people exceptionally talented in Discipline® enjoy routine and structure. They live by the order they create for their lives."[2]

High routine and structure through Discipline® is a lesser talent of mine in which I have not invested time or energy to improve. The thought of it literally drains me. When high Discipline® is needed to plan, launch, or implement a project, it is a signal for me to go to plan B, C, or D. Sometimes you must embrace your lesser talents to move forward, to get things done. At times like this, I have found it helpful to enlist the support of others with dominances in the talents/strengths needed. Understanding beyond your dominant talents is important as it helps you have a greater sense of your lesser talents.

Does it mean that you never have to actively engage your lesser talents? No, not at all. This is where the value of knowing your strengths allows you to lean into one of your more dominant talents to pair with your lesser talent(s) to complete tasks that call for that strength. To navigate or manage a weakness is best achieved by identifying one or two of your more dominant talents or strengths to fill in and compensate for what's needed. This can guide you with enlisting the support of other people on your team to get things done—people who possess talents that are not dominant for you. It is a great way to leverage your strengths to complete tasks with less stress and anxiety while working to achieve completion and success.

ASSESSMENTS ARE TOOLS TO REVEAL YOUR STRENGTHS

One of the best ways to identify your strengths is through personality assessments. They are excellent tools designed to measure your personality traits, characteristics, and behavioral tendencies. These types of assessments are based on psychological theories of personality and aim to provide insights into how you think, feel, and behave in various situations. They serve to help you and others better understand your unique and predictive behaviors.

I love assessments. They are fascinating tools to help you know yourself better. All assessments are not the same. The assessments used in my practice have been highly researched and vetted to determine if each one is a good fit for the Intentional Leadership Process System™. It is important to know the origin of the instrument and the efforts used to ensure inclusive and diverse openness is intentionally built in and reflected within the assessment. All assessments have some measure of bias because we all have biases. Finding those that make a conscious effort to minimize their biases are those of most interest for my practice.

The primary assessments used and administered by Dr. Helen Holton and Associates are as follows:

- Gallup CliftonStrengths® assessment
- Hogan Leadership Forecast Series and the Hogan 360 assessment
- Intercultural Development Inventory®
- The Maxwell DISC Method

Personality assessments are excellent tools to learn more about who you are by nature and nurture, inside and out. Think of it as your earthly DNA; it is unique to you and can assist and guide your leadership to reveal your optimal path to leadership success. Assessments can help you discover or affirm who you are and bring awareness to areas where you are spot-on in how you lead and where there is room for growth and improvement. They are excellent tools to support and augment your leadership development by assessing who you are beneath the surface. Those benefits alone make the assessments worth the investment.

There are various purposes for which you may want to consider using personality assessments. They are most often used for self-exploration, career guidance, employee selection, hiring at senior or executive levels, and team building. As a leader working to develop your team, assessments and their results are a piece of the puzzle to help you better understand the human behavioral element of the various members of your team. The value assessments can provide in driving your vision and those you lead into the future is worth the exploration.

Use assessments judiciously and in conjunction with other relevant information for more accurate interpretations. And be mindful of the role that biases—conscious and unconscious—can play in the development and interpretative measures used in determining personality traits and behavioral patterns. Personality can be assessed in multiple ways. Three key methods commonly used are self-reporting questionnaires, projective tests, and behavioral observations.

SELF-REPORTING QUESTIONNAIRES

Self-reporting questionnaires are one of the most widely used formats for psychometric assessments. They involve you answering a series of questions about yourself, your preferences, and behaviors. The most common ones use Likert scales where you are asked to numerically rate the extent to which you feel each question describes your thoughts, feelings, or behaviors.

They are easy to distribute and complete, tend to be cost effective, and provide you with helpful insights into behavior. The downside to be mindful of is the ability for respondents to not pay close attention, not fully understand what's being asked, or not answer truthfully. There may be an increase in unconscious biases like social desirability, whereby the desire to respond "politically correct" rather than truthfully may impair the accuracy of the instrument.

PROJECTIVE TESTS

Projective tests present you with ambiguous stimuli (e.g., abstract or vague images, objects, or words) and ask you to interpret or describe what you see. Your responses are believed to reveal hidden aspects or insights about your personality and ways of thinking.

There are limitations to these types of tests due to reliance on their interpretive nature and lack of a consistent or quantifiable way of scoring individual responses. One of the more well-known examples of a projective test is the Rorschach Inkblot Test.

BEHAVIORAL OBSERVATIONS

The behavioral observations method of personality assessment involves observing and documenting your behavior in specific situations to assess your personality traits. This method requires a greater investment of resources to include the time and having an experienced and qualified observer code the behavior. They can be a useful complement to self-reporting questionnaires to provide an external corroboration of behavior. However, the validity is contingent on the reliability of the responses in your self-report questionnaire.

When you know who you are at your best through your most dominant strengths, you're positioned for your greatest potential path to success. It is through the development of your talents that allows them to become your guiding strengths. Knowing yourself through your strengths is the result of the investment you make in your leadership development and professional growth.

In my program, we begin the coaching journey with an in-depth interview to get to know you as you know you. We then administer several assessments to identify your strengths, weaknesses, opportunities, and threats (S.W.O.T.) or derailers to your success. It's like a personal S.W.O.T. analysis. Through in-depth confidential debriefs of the assessment tools, we unpack your results together and begin a deeper dive exploring who you are at your best!

Through validated and reliable independent instruments, we coach and guide you to uncover, affirm, and develop who you are and how to navigate derailers to your success. Here is where we confront differences between how you may "actually" behave and the perceptions others may have of you. This is the beginning of our journey together to bring awareness and alignment of you as a stronger, more intentional leader. On purpose.

REFLECTION QUESTIONS AND NOTES

How much time do you spend investing in knowing yourself better, "warts and all"?

____

____

____

____

____

What do you do to continue to invest in the development of your strengths?

____

____

____

____

____

When is the last time you took an assessment to support your growth and development as a leader? When is the last time you looked at your results?

____

____

____

____

____

Have you ever sensed when you've taken a strength too far? What difference did you notice? How did it make you feel?

____

____

____

____

____

CHAPTER 7

LEVERAGING YOUR STRENGTHS TO LEAD

"Leadership is unlocking people's potential to become better."
—Bill Bradley, two-time NBA champion
and former US senator

When you develop and hone your strengths and skills to go from what you can do to what you are meant to do, you shift from career to purpose. This is a distinction to take notice of. It doesn't come by happenstance, and it is not a fluke out of left field. It requires your commitment and, more importantly, your intention.

A colleague and dear friend who is a gifted poet penned the poem, "Leading with Strength," that beautifully captures a vision of what it can mean when you lead with your strengths. It is heartwarming and brings to life what it means to be intentional about your leadership and to lead as a servant leader. It touched my heart and spoke to the universality of servant leaders who lead with intention. I share it with you with the poet's permission. May it inspire you and move you forward to strengthen your leadership with intention, and on purpose.

> **"Leading with Strength"** *by Peter Colwell*
>
> *Your strength as a leader will often depend*
> *On what kind of message you're willing to send.*
> *At first sign of trouble, will you break? Will you bend?*
> *Stay true to your values right to the end?*
>
> *Will you lead with your heart*
> *And not just your head?*
> *First the horse,* **THEN** *the cart...*
> *Will you lead... or be led?*
>
> *At the end of the day, a leader must* **care**.
> *A leader must* **do** *and a leader must* **dare**.
> *A leader must* **learn** *and a leader must* **share**.
>
> *For knowledge is nothing until we give it away*
> *Empowering others to* **seize the day**!
> *Each moment presents us with chances anew*
> *To draw forth in others the* **BEST** *they can do!*

SEEDS OF STRENGTH PLANTED

Dr. Mildred McKinney was a pivotal person who poured into me and demonstrated a future unknown to me as a young college student. She was a professor at Morgan State University (MSU), who was a major influencer in my life. She passed away in 2005. I regret not being able to personally share with her the tremendous impact she had on my life.

As a sophomore at MSU in 1978, I participated in an extracurricular activity to serve as a peer counselor. The program was housed in the department of social work and was created and led by Professor McKinney. Students served as peer ambassadors and guides and were trained to assist faculty and staff with the onboarding experience of incoming freshmen.

Our training consisted of instruction in coaching, role-play, and honest dialogue. She taught by example, modeling and living inclusive behaviors. Dr. McKinney practiced what she preached and fostered a sense of belonging in us all. She didn't tell us what to do but guided us through a well-developed process.

Today, I understand the value of the one-on-one courageous coaching conversations we, as students, were fortunate enough to have with Dr. McKinney. They caused me to think more deeply in search of answers that led to growth and learning beyond the superficial. Being absorbed in this level of deeper engagement with professors and peers was captivating with high energy. It wasn't referred to as coaching then.

I had no idea, at the time, how this experience would come full circle in life. Dr. McKinney planted seeds that are in full bloom today. It began with an exploration into new and different ways of engaging people and being of support and value to their progress and success. She planted seeds of confidence, a pursuit of excellence, curiosity to reach into the unknown, and a passion to serve others for their greater good.

It's important to identify and acknowledge the people in your life who add value and richness to who you are as a leader. The love, guidance, and support Dr. McKinney provided by planting seeds within me were worth the effort. She was a teacher, mentor, and friend for many years. My experience with her made me a believer in giving people their flowers while they are still living.

Dr. McKinney saw strengths in me early in life that were nowhere on my radar beyond the joy and fulfillment derived from doing the work. In retrospect, serving as a peer counselor and earning three elective credits brought a sense of purpose and achievement to my life that resonated with strengths unknown at the time. They were still seeds deeply planted.

I recognized not long ago that I planted seeds in someone else at the same time seeds were being planted in me by Dr. McKinney, making this a beautiful circular moment. A woman approached me at an event and shared with me how we met at MSU when I was her peer counselor. She shared with me the impact I had made on her life and how she continued to follow my career path and accomplishments. I was amazed that she remembered me decades later from our days of being undergrads. It also affirmed the power of learning to leverage your strengths to lead well.

The remembrance of the experience remained dormant in my memory until writing this book. Those seeds sprouted, took root, and blossomed. I learned to leverage my strengths, which ultimately led to the best career shift ever—one in alignment with who I am at my best.

I gained a better sense of myself then; however, I wasn't mature enough to fully appreciate the value of the seeds planted by Dr. McKinney. The blessing is that the seeds were planted in good, fertile soil; they just needed time to grow and produce a harvest. The aperture of my lens was widened to see other possibilities to pursue. As I became aware of my strengths, those seeds began to germinate, grow, and produce a rich harvest fertilized with intention.

Every experience you encounter—good or bad—is never wasted. All your experiences leave an imprint in your life of who you are. We're pretty quick to recognize the bad and invite our inner critic to gloat over our mistakes and wrong directions. We don't always recognize the connections and power of our strengths and how they work for our success.

You may have a hunch or gut instinct of who you are becoming through your strengths. It may or may not be who you are at your best without further earnest exploration. Our weaknesses are a part of who we are as well. What we do with them matters; however, we must first identify them. An easy way to become aware of your weaknesses is to gauge how they impact you physically, emotionally, and mentally.

STRENGTHS LEVERAGED

Learning to leverage your strengths to bring greater joy, satisfaction, and fulfillment to your life is an intentional act available to you as a leader to better direct your life. It begins with the awareness of your strengths followed by the development of them. It takes time and active engagement to have your dominant talents truly become your signature strengths.

I'm reminded of the journey of my longtime friend, colleague, mentee, and now executive of a burgeoning nonprofit organization she founded. Dawnita Brown and I met in church in the late 1990s. Our relationship began as mentor-mentee and quickly blossomed from there. Dawnita grew up in a culture that believed a "good government job" with benefits was a prize worthy of pursuit. It also limited her thinking about possibilities beyond.

After nine years of federal service, she made the bold decision to resign because she was no longer happy where she was in terms of using her God-given gifts, skills, and talents. An awakening of curiosity was occurring within her that organically challenged her to pursue more. She shared with me "I was just there, working and making good money, and feeling very stuck. I knew there was more for me; I just didn't know how to get it." This is an example of how your strengths intrinsically reveal themselves and drive you to take action, to leverage the best of who you know yourself to be.

Timing is everything, and when the awareness of your strengths intersects with the pursuit of your passion and purpose, a shift of alignment happens. Dawnita left her "good government job" to pursue alignment with her passion, purpose, and strengths. Not only did she leave the security of employment and a paycheck, but she learned how to step into her strengths and leverage them.

Dawnita ventured into several roles before finding her sweet spot. It began by leaning into her natural talents that, at the onset of her career, were not in alignment. She's a very gifted, talented, innovative, and visionary creator of graphic design and publications. She went from being a federal government professional to public school teacher to part-time executive assistant to Peace Corps volunteer to her current role as the founder of a thriving nonprofit organization. The journey was marked with dull flat roads, deep curves of uncertainty, and uphill climbs that led to unforeseen destinations. The one constant was the growth and development of her strengths with some guidance through coaching.

> *"You challenged me to broaden my scope with a more holistic vision of what's possible. More than anything, you coached me on how to be more intentional about the use of my gifts, skills, and talents. When life threw me a curveball and shifted my life plans to become a full-time caregiver to my mother in an instant, it was through my strengths and resilience that I was able to rebound and transition forward. You changed the trajectory of my life."*
>
> —Dawnita Brown, Founder of Hey Caregiver!™ and The Binti Circle

LIFELONG LEARNING IS FOREVER

We are created as relational beings designed to continually grow, learn, and be in communion with each other. There's no such notion as reaching a point where you feel like there's nothing else for you to learn to make you a better person. Change is the only constant in this life we encounter. When you believe you no longer need to consider change or growth as something viable to your life is when you begin to die. Death has finality. If you're alive, it is an opportunity for you to grow and become better, more of who you were created to be.

When you live your life from a perspective of continual curiosity, you exhibit a heightened degree of excitement about your experiences. The people you meet along your journey become encounters that beg for self-reflection. We all have something to teach and learn from one another. Spending time alone with your own ideas and thoughts opens you up to new possibilities for growth and development. Who you are today may very well be the best person you've ever been. Your being here right now reading this book also speaks to your desire for continued learning and growth.

The awareness of your strengths is the key that opens the door to intentional leadership. Resilience and well-being are the other pillars that round out the intentional leadership signature process, which is where we are headed next. If you've made it this far, give yourself a high-five! You're on your way to becoming a more intentional leader.

REFLECTION QUESTIONS AND NOTES

How does your current role/position as a leader drain your energy?

____

____

____

____

____

What challenges confront you most in the course of your day? How do you recognize them? What do you do about it?

____

____

____

____

____

Name five people who push you forward in pursuit of your **dreams. When is** the last time you reached out to connect **with them?**

____

____

____

____

____

____

What's it worth for you to explore how you can improve **your leadership** for better results?

____

____

____

____

____

RESILIENCE

"In the face of adversity, true leaders find strength in resilience and turn challenges into opportunities for growth."

—Barack Obama, former US president

You can activate your resilience and not know it. Resilience isn't something we're born with; it's something you build throughout your life. Resilience is a skillset that can move you from struggling to surviving to thriving. To gain command of resilience in your life as a tool begins with a conscious recognition of it, especially when it's actively engaged and present to you in the moment or shortly thereafter. It's another layer of awareness. Think of it as something you call upon on purpose when stress, upset, or disruption interrupts your flow.

In other words, resilience is very much about being intentional. Your conscious awareness of resilience is your invitation to develop and build it for yourself. Resilience is your personal power source to get you through life's upsets and setbacks and get you back on track with an upward trajectory towards your success. The journey to intentional leadership is anchored by your conscious willingness and ability to build and practice resilience.

It is a choice you make on purpose before you find yourself in crisis or distress. That's what makes it intentional. It doesn't always happen this way; sometimes it's your instinct that leads you there and not intention. Think about it like this—there may be times in life when your resilience is driven by survival.

As a teenager, I struggled with the challenges of moving through life as a part of the non-dominant culture in America—female and African American. Coming of age in the 1970s, living in a predominantly white neighborhood, and attending predominantly white schools was a lot to swallow in the most challenging years of human development. In my search to find meaning, value, and a sense of self, I stumbled upon a message of hope for being different and being okay. It was my first taste of building resilience; I just didn't know it at the time. I didn't know what imposter syndrome was then either.

Being in the fifth grade and the only Black child in the fifth grade at my school was nothing short of a glaring difference among my fellow classmates. Challenges included, but were not limited to, indulging the curiosities about our differences like hair care, sunburning, and cultural dietary delicacies. Finding common ground to forge relationships was interesting, informative, and occasionally mean-spirited. Trying to fit in and be accepted in my environment was a way to numb the pain and isolation I sometimes felt from being different. It also taught me to be strong and self-accepting of myself when teased and taunted by others.

American author, clinical social worker, and psychotherapist Virginia Satir's prose, "I Am Me," connected, comforted, and clarified what it meant to be okay with me—just as I was. She wrote this while working with a troubled teenager who was looking to find acceptance of herself. I captured it in my journal, and it became an anchor for this mixed-up teenager in search of herself. It affirmed my uniqueness and difference as normal for me. The following is an excerpt of her prose:

I Am Me

In all the world, there is no one exactly like me. There are persons who have some parts like me, but no one adds up exactly like me. Therefore, everything that comes out of me is authentically mine because I alone choose it.

> *I own everything about me, My body including every-*
> *thing it does; My mind including all its thoughts and ideas;*
> *My eyes including the images of all they behold; My feelings*
> *whatever they may be … anger, joy, frustration, love, disap-*
> *pointment, excitement; My Mouth and all the words that*
> *come out of it polite, sweet or rough, correct or incorrect; My*
> *Voice loud or soft. And all my actions, whether they be to*
> *others or to myself.*
>
> *I own my fantasies, my dreams, my hopes, my fears. I own*
> *all my triumphs and successes, all my failures and mistakes.*
> *Because I own all of me I can become intimately acquainted*
> *with me. By doing so I can love me and be friendly with me*
> *in all parts. I can then make it possible for all of me to work*
> *in my best interests.… .*
>
> *I am me and I am okay.*

I'd not read it in decades, and when I stumbled across it in a shoebox of memories, it immediately became clear that at the time her writing appeared in my life, I was building resilience without even knowing what it was. It was a tool, an anchor to help me face the difficulties of growing up different. It validated me and that I mattered. It was my first experience with resilience.

Building resilience is not always a conscious or active power that you put in place to protect you; empower you; or propel you to think, be, or do differently to keep you anchored and moving forward. I learned throughout my life how to be okay with me. It didn't happen overnight. Re-reading the full text of "I Am Me" was an endearing reminder of a lifeline that helped me to cope and choose life by way of building resilience.

I'm no longer a teenager, and what I know, as an adult, is that resilience is an anchor to keep you grounded and moving forward in spite of your internal and external critics, naysayers, and haters. When you actively engage your resilience to achieve what you want for your life as a leader on purpose is what makes your leadership intentional.

CHAPTER 8

GRATITUDE IS RESILIENCE

"I have been sustained throughout my life by three saving graces—my family, my friends, and a faith in the power of resilience and hope."

—Elizabeth Edwards, American attorney, author, and healthcare activist

Life is a continual journey of connections to help you evolve and grow into living your life full of joy, hope, peace, love, and gratitude. Gratitude is not an automatic given just because you're living. When you discover gratitude as a strength, it makes the unfortunate more than bearable; it makes it conquerable. Gratitude is a mindset that equips leaders for the long haul. Gratitude adds to your reservoir of resilience and strengthens your leadership in good times and challenging times.

Disappointments and detours in life happen all the time, and being grateful for them is usually not the first thing that comes to mind. Have you ever found yourself asking "Why me? What did I do to deserve this?" The "this" is often the challenge, difficulty, or derailment life presents you. I can imagine how you felt. I've felt the same way and have asked myself some of the same questions you've asked…and some are still unanswered.

Life's not always easy or pleasant, and your life experiences don't always have answers—at least not the ones you want to hear. The ups and downs, triumphs and defeats, and everything else in between we live through can sometimes make you feel like you want to stop and get off the merry-go-round of misery, disappointments, and broken dreams. Gratitude is the balm that can soothe the pains and heal the hurts of life, even those that may seem too great to bear or that seem to never go away.

It is a blessing when you wake up to the dawn of a new day. You are blessed if you have a roof overhead, a warm bed to sleep in, and food to eat. Do you live with daily aches and pains to remind you of how blessed you are even when they interfere with living the way you think you should? Have you ever experienced something awful that changed your life forever? Interrupted the dreams and plans you had for your life? I have.

Resilience taught me to survive what seemed to be the end of my life at one time or another. How do you find the courage and strength to face painful, difficult, and unexplainable realities? Gratitude is a life force that can open you to new perspectives and ways of being. Gratitude teaches you to see and live in the silver lining of the clouds in your life. When you encounter traumatic life-changing experiences that come out of nowhere, it's gratitude that elevates you to a higher plane. It opens the path that leads your life into the overflow of daily blessings. A spirit of gratitude helps you live brighter days even when the sun is not shining.

A bump on my arm the size of a pea launched an avalanche of physical, emotional, and mental challenges that began in my twenties. As a healthy young professional woman on the rise, this needed to be addressed and resolved. Quickly. That was another lesson learned. The bottom line is this: Most of us have lived through something that changed our lives dramatically, traumatically, or not the way we ever thought it would. And that is okay. It is what it is. My outcome led to a few failed attempts at remedies followed by shock therapy, which consisted of a ten-day regimen of prednisone, a steroid drug prescribed under the care of two doctors. The plan was to shock my system and stop the intrusive spread of the abnormality throughout my body. If you don't know about prednisone, by all accounts, it's a life-saving drug used for a multitude of seasonal and chronic health conditions. In my case, it created a rare and uncommon side-effect reaction that changed my life forever.

From 1988 to 1991, I lived in pain twenty-four hours a day and seven days a week. Walking on canes and crutches, living on medical disability income provided by my job, and taking prescription medications to address the deep pain within that never went away was my existence. The turnaround breakthrough came on January 10, 1991.

It happened while in post-op recovery after my first total hip replacement at the age of thirty. As I awakened from surgery, lying in bed with all sorts of tubes, hoses, pumps, and IVs and still groggy from the anesthesia, my first conscious thought was that the deep, nagging pain within my body was gone. The light at the end of a long, dark tunnel was visible. It gave me the ability to see all I had endured over the past few years. Overcome with gratitude and the power of resilience is what got me through. It brought tears of joy filled with forward progress and gratitude.

Life is full of twists and turns, hopes and fears, victories and defeats. Resilience isn't something we're born with; it's something we build throughout our lives. When you consciously connect with the power of resilience, it's a game changer. Resilience is a power that helps you persevere and push through the upsets and derailers of your life to pursue what you want for your life. Resilience teaches you how to live strong on purpose with power and intention.

When you build resilience, it keeps you from checking out of the game of life. Gratitude elevates and empowers you to play full-out in your life—to live on the other side of "Yes!" Resilience keeps you humble and grateful for all things great and small, within and beyond ordinary living. Gratitude fills you with indescribable joy, hope, and optimism for the here and now and what's next to come.

On Monday, October 12, 2015, I had hip surgery number seven. I went in without pain or any visible signs of a problem. As a veteran of hip surgeries by then, my disappointment was not as earth-shattering as it could have been. I'd been here before. What made this time different was to learn that I was a walking time bomb, waiting to explode and cause major damage to my body and possibly my ability to walk again.

After a few years of observation and tracking of the intervention to make me as whole as possible, the surgery was declared a success. The other side of success was that I've lived in pain ever since. Some days are better than others, and I've learned to count every day as a gift. Having endured multiple hip surgeries and still walking, most of the time unassisted, on my own two feet, is nothing short of God's grace and the power of resilience and gratitude.

This wasn't always my story or truth; however, today, it is. What began as a response to a health abnormality transitioned into multiple hip surgeries that have dramatically altered my life. I'm grateful for every one of them. The experience taught me that I'm stronger than I would have ever imagined and have lived through what seemed impossible. God's grace awakened the power of resilience and the priceless value of deep, abiding gratitude. My favorite book is the Holy Bible. It's God's love letter to me. In 1 Thessalonians 5:16 and 18 are conscious reminders to "Rejoice always...give thanks in all circumstances...."

Learning to give thanks for the good, the bad, and the indifferent experiences will transform your life into one filled with unimaginable joy and blessings. Fill your cup with gratitude, and it will never be empty. Open the window of your soul for your countenance to shine from inside you into a world that needs to see and feel more joy, peace, hope, love, and gratitude.

Resilience is a reason to rejoice always and to give thanks in all ways. I share this very personal story because what people see of you on the outside is not always the full picture of what you have been through in life or where you are headed. Resilience can make all the difference in the world; don't ever underestimate its power.

REFLECTION QUESTIONS AND NOTES

What keeps you moving forward when you're going through life's storms?

____

____

____

____

____

____

How do you prepare yourself to confront disruption to your leadership?

____

____

____

____

____

____

CHAPTER 9

ANCHORS MAKE YOU STRONGER

"We can endure almost anything if we are centered, if we have some focus in our life. You can endure if you have an anchor."
—Rev. Dr. Renita J. Weems, PhD, American writer, clergy, and motivational speaker

What does it mean to be anchored? Is it possible to really become stronger when you're going through struggles? Like you, I've faced a struggle or two throughout life (as I've illustrated at various points along our way). You don't always win, and defeat can sometimes be gut-wrenching. It's interesting how we can allow our victories to be overshadowed or minimized by the struggles, setbacks, and seemingly insurmountable challenges we've overcome. Your victories add value to help you maneuver the next upset that darkens your path. Acknowledging and celebrating your success over struggles strengthens your resolve when the next struggle shows up.

There are times when matters that pique your curiosity draw you in to explore more deeply and increase your knowledge, learning, and understanding about it. There's an interrelated connection among your struggles, strengths, and success. What do I mean? When you know your strengths and invest in them, that's an action that increases your potential to be an intentional leader, leading at your best. However, as a treasured mentor and anointed woman of faith told me long ago, "With new level come new 'devils.'" In secular terminology, think about your rise to leadership. Did you encounter new challenges, upsets, or struggles? Of course, you did…if you were putting your all into becoming the leader you know you have the potential to be.

Confronting struggles lets you know you're on the right path to impact the lives of others through the gifts, talents, and strengths that only you can bring to the world. When you're living into your passion and purpose, your haters are out there to challenge you and take you down. This is where anchors make you stronger and more resilient to withstand and overcome the battles that will arise. You might get knocked down, but you won't get knocked out.

THE BEAUTY AND POWER OF WORDS

I love a good play on words. Whether it's a challenging clue in a crossword puzzle, rhythmic lyrics in a melodic and soulful song, or a treatise on surviving against the odds, it deepens understanding and perspective. Words, phrases, and statements can easily spark discussion or debate on struggles, strengths, and success. When you make a deeper connection to the language people use with you or about you, you are better able to be more intentional about your responses. You can stand taller and build others up instead of retaliating by tearing them down because of your choice of words.

A common approach used to refresh and deepen your interpretation of life and understanding of words and relationships is to turn to a generally accepted authoritative source like the dictionary. Dictionaries have evolved to be more diverse and inclusive of its definitions to reflect cultural shifts and nuances of our modern age. They used to be rather large and voluminous books you pulled from a shelf in a library or your home. Do you remember those days? Thank goodness that today you can scan thousands of pages with an easy tap on an app on your smartphone to begin an inquiry.

The beauty and convenience of technological advances means that a device, i.e. smartphone, tablet, or some other portable technology, allows you to instantly gain a better understanding of words and language and their usage just about anywhere with an internet connection. I'm a leader, mindful of the words I use. The context, audience, and environment matter when you are focused on being intentional about the language you use. Check the content of your message and the words you use; doing so can make or break the intent of your message.

For example, a word like *struggle* has multiple ways it can be used. The very first definition listed under the word *struggle* at dictionary.com is "to contend with an adversary or opposing force."[1] Wow! Immediately upon reading the definition, it registered powerful feelings. It touched my thinking mind, vulnerable heart, and anchored spirit. This is not to take anything from the other definitions listed. They all spoke in varying ways of how we come to understand words in the context of how we live life and as leaders. That first meaning hit a chord that solidly landed and urged further exploration.

Living in and through struggles is a very real part of life. Some of us do it better than others, and sometimes, we succumb to the wiles of an adversary or our inner critic and lose our way in confronting the struggle. But when you are anchored by resilience, it keeps you from falling while finding your power within to move forward like intentional leaders do.

SELF-IDENTIFICATION AS AN ANCHOR

How we identify ourselves has a direct impact on how we understand and respond to the world around us. It also reflects how other people may perceive and respond to you. Your self-identification is shaped throughout your life. As you experience life, develop, and mature, you are also building the foundation that anchors you, that keeps you grounded. The more open, honest, and transparent you are about who you are influences the kind of leader you become. It's your choice to decide the kind of leader you want to be.

Our identities usually begin to form at home in our family life and upbringing. In this family of origin, we are taught, told, and molded by what our parents (or caregivers) say, do, and model. Do you recall hearing, as a child, a grown-up telling you "Do as I say, not as I do. I'm the parent/adult"?

This is a statement of conflict to a child with the potential to adversely affect rational reasoning as an adult. As children, much of the defense mechanisms we employ are instinctual, subconscious, and learned behavior from our surroundings and influences. However, in the broader reality of your life, if you grew up in a loving and supportive family and community, you understood the hierarchy of identities and roles between adults and children. This seemingly simple phrase, "Do as I say, not as I do," taught me valuable and lifelong lessons about culture, belonging, discipline, and leadership.

Growing up as an African American female in the 1960s is the foundational lens that shapes the narrative. The single-digit years of my life began in predominantly Black neighborhoods in Baltimore City. By the age of ten, our family moved to the suburbs and integrated a predominantly white neighborhood as the first Black, single-headed household on our block. It was an up-close and personal experience of being different and confronting challenges that would move with me throughout life. Neighborhoods and communities are not synonymous.

To be visually identified as different was my first introduction to diversity and cultural differences in the fifth grade. Not fully understanding what that meant then became a subject of interest and curiosity that continues to be actively pursued. The shared stories of survival and success over struggles using strengths and resilience is part of my backstory and part of the "why" of the work Dr. Helen Holton and Associates is engaged in today.

During your young adult years, when you're not tethered as tightly to your parent(s) or caregiver(s) who raised you opens you to opportunities of curiosity about what your life experiences have revealed. The views, opinions, and perspectives of family invite your personal critical exploration to find your own way in the world. This is where culture begins to present the similarities and differences that unite and divide us as a community.

The subjective and objective aspects of who we are reflect the conscious and unconscious biases with which we live. They show up through our feelings, thoughts, words, and actions that determine and influence the kind of person and leader you are or are becoming. The less conscious you are of how the world receives and perceives you can create a disconnect between the person you believe yourself to be and how you show up. This is a struggle for leaders who do not invest in their own self-work, professionally and personally.

Your self-identity is your unique imprint in the world. How you understand your identity as you continue to shape, grow, and refine your leadership builds your self-identity as an anchor. There are multiple anchors intentional leaders build to be resilient because life's upsets, setbacks, or disruptions don't have a one-size-fits-all resolution. Building a reservoir of resilience with different anchors keeps you moving forward to what's next for your leadership.

FAITH AS AN ANCHOR

Having a faith or belief as an anchor is something you believe in and accept as your truth that you know is greater than and beyond yourself. For me, that's God. Whether you believe in God or not, what I've learned from working with leaders, especially successful ones, is that recognizing a spiritual force or a higher power is instrumental in their life and success as a leader.

The tumultuous years of adolescence leading to adulthood are usually filled with what you might consider the awakening of how you shape your own personal views and attitudes about the world. This is typically the stage in life where your spiritual beliefs are explored the most and begin to take root in developing your adult personhood.

Having researched, explored, and experienced various faith traditions was the guidance to the definitive conclusions about what I was willing to accept or leave behind, love, tolerate, or reject. When you become clear on what you believe and what anchors your faith, you are better positioned to choose practices that sustain you through life. The process develops your underlying conviction that supports your character through life's struggles and successes. This conscious awareness and acceptance of your belief system as a tool to build resilience may involve beyond earthly life-changing events.

Church has been a part of my life for as long as I can remember. I am anchored and solidly grounded in the Christian faith and my love of God. I am an itinerant elder, an ordained minister, in the African Methodist Episcopal Church. The clarity of God's omnipotent presence in life is an affirmed truth I own and strive to live out as an ambassador of love.

When the ways of the world wreak havoc on my earthly perceptions, the default is a simple question for me, WWJD or "What would Jesus do?" Some years ago, in the early days when rubber wristbands were popular, these four letters, WWJD, became an anchor that supported success through struggles I had encountered and overcome. Having faith or a belief system as an anchor is a powerful tool of resilience to have in your pocket.

The choices we make about the root causes of our struggles in life are solely our responsibility. They have the power to determine our outcomes. Whether you believe in heaven or hell, good versus evil, or nothing at all as it pertains to your life in the here and now or the ever after is totally up to you. This is the power you have over your life.

As a Christian, it led to my belief that the struggles of our lives are the attempts of the adversary or enemy to steal, kill, and destroy your joy. So, when I went to the dictionary, looked up the word *struggle*, and found that the first definition referenced the word *adversary*,[5] this was an immediate reminder and affirmation for me that God is an anchor, always and in all ways, especially in times of struggle.

God strengthens you through your struggles, fears, and stubbornness with never-ending love and support. There was a time in life when I was an easy conquest for the enemy. I kept a false belief that fear was greater than love and that giving in or giving up was a better choice than fighting back. Now, I fight back undergirded by my faith.

I invite you to pause for an introspective reflection to consider the power source to which you ascribe. The bottom line is that when you are anchored in a power, force, or source greater than you, struggles are not as bad as they could be. And resilience is your ability to more easily rebound from them.

As a member of the ministerial staff at church, my responsibilities include visiting the sick and shut-in. We visit to encourage them, pray for and with them, give them hope, and remind them of the power of their faith. Having witnessed improved health and miraculous turnarounds of church members challenged by serious and terminal conditions is a sign of the power of faith and resilience. Leveraging your strengths with resilience when serving others can make what seems impossible possible.

Before, learning how to identify needs, develop strategies, and build resilience to fight back and move forward against the struggles and setbacks of others would not have been possible without being anchored. We all have upsets and disappointments that hit us when we least expect them. It's what we do after we've been knocked down that makes the difference.

Deepening my relationship with God and learning to build spiritual muscles and to trust God to fight my battles saved my life. The most powerful attack against my life was an affront to my physical health. Our health is the greatest wealth we have.

Without good health or the best health you can be in, your hopes, dreams, and future may be compromised and require modifications to reach fulfillment.

Your challenges become more complicated and the probability of optimal outcomes diminished. Whatever condition your body is in, when you decide how you'll treat it and live within it, to an extent, determines how far in life you will go. What I thought was the beginning of my end strengthened and prepared me for bigger battles later in life.

Confronted by life-altering challenges that leave an indelible imprint on your life produces incredible life lessons, wisdom, and witness. As you continue to strengthen your walk in your faith or belief, your resilience grows as well. Thanks to the physical, emotional, and spiritual attacks to my body, mind, and faith, the outcome became an anchor that keeps me on solid footing like never before. I am stronger than I've ever been.

Like the Apostle Paul, when life exposes your weakness is when you can experience your greatest strength. That's being anchored. The metaphorical thorn in your life is not always removed at your command. Sometimes it manifests itself physically as pain and suffering of your flesh. Like Jacob, who wrestled through the night and was left with a limp for life as a reminder, I, too, have scars and impairments to remind me. They keep me humble and hopeful. I am not ashamed of my faith. God is the anchor that makes me an intentional leader and my leadership resilient.

ANCHOR YOUR LEADERSHIP IN RESILIENCE

There is a way to prepare for and confront the struggles of life before they come. It's not easy, but it's so worth it. I'm sure you've encountered challenges that came out of left field and knocked you down. Knocked down isn't knocked out, and getting back up is a choice. When you have anchors in life that keep you grounded, getting back up is an easier choice to make.

Think about the people in your life who don't get back up. They yield to their disruptions for various reasons. In leadership, you must learn to make choices and not excuses if you want to optimize your success. You've got to be willing to get out of your comfort zone and take some risks. In pursuit of your dreams and passions, I'm sure you've encountered decision points along the way that either took you higher or knocked you down. Don't allow your knockdowns to take you out of pursuing what you want for your life. In the words of motivational speaker Dr. Willie Jolley, "A setback is a setup for a comeback."

Resilience isn't something we're born with, and most of us don't make the connection between leadership success and resilience. Building resilience is no different than working out at the gym to build your body and improve your health. Think of resilience as a muscle to be exercised and used to be of greatest value. The change begins on the inside before it's recognized on the outside. It's truly a mind/body/spirit connection.

It doesn't happen overnight nor does preparing to run a marathon. However, if you consistently work at it over time, you will become more resilient and better able to withstand your trials. As a leader, the higher your leadership rises, so will your challenges and struggles that seek to circumvent your ascent. Bouncing back from setbacks isn't easy, but it is achievable.

The depth and breadth of our struggles are not always visible for others to see nor are they meant to be. When you share your stories of setbacks and struggles not to gain sympathy or pity but to own the battles you face, it allows you to identify them by name. Naming your struggles out loud shifts your energy and willingness to confront and overcome them. It also helps you to identify your allies who will support you as you go through.

Your allies encourage you in ways that open you up to embrace what you're going through. To see and believe that you can endure whatever it takes for you to get through to the other side of adversity is to be resilient and anchored. When you model resilience as a leader, you help your team understand that it's not about you—it's about how you add value to them. You give them a perspective to embrace about what intentional leadership looks like for the team and the organization.

REFLECTION QUESTIONS AND NOTES

What anchors do you have to keep you resilient and grounded through your struggles?

____

____

____

____

____

How does the relationship among your strengths, struggles, and successes influence your leadership?

____

____

____

____

____

CHAPTER 10

BUILD YOUR RESERVOIR OF RESILIENCE

"Life isn't meant to be easy, it's meant to be lived. Sometimes happy, other times rough...But with every up and down you learn lessons that make you strong."
—Charlie Brown, American comic strip character

Evolving into a niche as an executive leadership coach, providing coaching, training, and consulting services to leaders, teams, and organizations, is transformative work. It's engaging, fulfilling, and in alignment with my strengths. And yes, sometimes it makes me want to pull my hair out and scream. It's a healthy tension to experience and from which to grow. The combination of formal education and training, lived experiences, and earned expertise to do what I love was not an accident or an overnight success. It is an ongoing intentional process that continues to shape and refine the results it produces. Resilience is the force that keeps me moving forward when the going gets tough.

Doubt, fears, and failures are a very real part of life and leadership. As a leader, they can impede your success as much as they can fuel it. Knowing yourself innately; intimately; and how you most naturally think, feel, and behave is powerful. We each have personality traits and ways of being that shape who we are and reveal our strengths and weaknesses. When you are in tune with your strengths and weaknesses, you're in a much better position to move through the curveballs life throws your way with greater success than failure. The deciding factor is your willingness to do the work. It doesn't happen by osmosis.

Developing a conscious awareness of your resilience teaches you how to maneuver your comebacks from upsets, missteps, and life happening beyond your control. Your power to activate your resilience in the moment to best serve you as the leader is not by accident; it's with intention. It puts you further ahead in achieving your desired outcomes despite your challenges and disappointments along the way. Does it mean you get everything right and never have moments of doubt and failures with which to contend? Absolutely not. Sometimes your greatest growth is experienced through your failures. Consider it as the fail forward principle.

There have been hiccups and missteps along the way with highs and lows to keep life real. They've made the journey rough sometimes and richly rewarding at other times. Resilience is a constant asset that's gotten me through the best of times and the worst. It can do the same for you. The struggle is real for solopreneurs, boutique businesses, and C-suite executives. Building and learning to lean into your resilience can be pivotal, especially in the early days of a new role, industry, or career.

The power of resilience begins with your awareness of it. It's connected to how you think, respond to your thoughts, and formulate your perspectives. The perspectives you attach to the myriad of ways adversity shows up for you is where your opportunities to build and practice resilience exist. Developing a cadre of tools to choose from and apply in different situations reduces anxiety, helps you get unstuck, and allows you to take action sooner rather than later.

TOOLS FOR BUILDING YOUR RESERVOIR OF RESILIENCE

Here are a few tools you can use to begin to build your reservoir of resilience.

Establish Anchors

The flow of life is not always smooth. Life throws you curveballs and fast pitches that you are not always ready, equipped, or prepared to receive. Tapping into your source of faith, belief, or inspiration with regularity makes going to that source more familiar and natural when faced with a crisis, setback, upset, or disruption. Life happens, storms come, and it's good to be anchored. Practice and spend time strengthening your anchor(s). Your anchor refers to a force or power greater than yourself and humanity (as we discussed in the previous chapter).

It's also something you can develop and practice individually and collectively in community with others.

Know Thyself

How often do you spend time tuning into you? Spending alone time, reflective time, all about "you" time is important to allow you to engage and dive deeper into you. This is essential as you grow and evolve. It supports you in cultivating and maintaining a healthy sense of self-awareness. Being true to yourself heightens your senses when fear, anger, or despair are lurking in your reality.

Self-awareness helps you know the difference between your needs and your wants. It alerts you when you need to reach out to someone for guidance, assistance, and/or support. You become more in-tune with the subtle clues on your horizon and are able to address them sooner than later. As Shakespeare said, "To thine own self be true."

Journaling is a wonderful way to get in touch with your feelings and emotions through your life experiences. It's almost like having a non-verbal conversation with yourself in a reflective and impactful way. I recommend journaling with pen and paper versus typing on a computer, tablet, or phone. When you write by hand as opposed to typing, you engage more complex motor and cognitive processes, which helps encode information in your memory more effectively.

Love Yourself

Loving yourself by making time and space for self-care is important to your work-life balance and overall well-being.

It's about your physical, mental, and emotional care—your state of being. When adversity strikes, the stronger your overall health, the greater your ability to be resilient enough to withstand challenges and bounce back. You matter. When you intentionally develop a love affair with yourself, the return is always on the upside.

Activate Your "A" Team

Close family members, friends, colleagues, and others whom you trust and believe have your back are the people who make up your "A" team. This intimate group of people is available to you because they love, respect, and genuinely care about your well-being. They serve as a sounding board and listening ear to give you open, honest, and constructive feedback to help you "feed forward" in the face of your challenges and obstacles when needed or requested. They are there to help catch you when you get knocked down and help you to regroup and move forward. If you have a personal advisory board (PAB) and/or personal pit crew (PPC), as explained later in this chapter, these are groups that can be considered as part of your "A" team.

I used to be one of those people who didn't want to bother the people on my "A" team when I needed them most. I allowed my inner critic or saboteur to have me believe they were too busy or that my issue wasn't important enough to bother them. The biggest myth I told myself is that I could handle it alone. Don't allow your inner critic to sabotage your leadership when disruptions, detours, and crises beyond your control park on your doorstep.

We are created as relational beings. We really do need each other to survive. Identify the people you want to enroll as part of your "A" team network. Deepen your relationship with them by investing time to nurture and develop it. Don't wait until you're knee-deep or overhead in counterproductive ways that interfere with the effectiveness of your leadership and your life.

Avoid Landmines of Your Mind

The tricks your saboteur, or your inner critic, plays on you can cause you to…

- Jump to conclusions without good data or facts;
- Play the self-blame game;
- Place the cause of your problems on people or things external to you;
- Assume that what others think about you is true when it's usually false; and/or
- Live in a mindset of generalities, making "everything" and "always" as well as "never" and "nothing" statements and explanations about something that warrants more.

When you allow your mind to fall on the landmines of life, you subject yourself to emotional stressors of anger, guilt, anxiety, sadness, embarrassment, shame, and more. These emotional responses can lead you to self-sabotage or unintentionally bringing hurt or harm to others. Before jumping to conclusions, slow down, pause, and examine the evidence upon which you are basing your conclusions. Practicing mindfulness, active listening, and non-judgmental engagement are ways to mitigate falling prey to landmines of your mind.

When You Fall Down, Get Up!

If at first you don't succeed, get up and go for it again. We all fall down in life, come up short, or miss the mark more than once. Falling down is an opportunity to reach out and connect to get back up. No one is perfect, and everything you do doesn't always yield the intended outcome you may have thought it would. That's life. Seeing your failures, setbacks, and upsets for what they are without added commentary can oftentimes make getting back up more palatable.

Life is about making choices. From the moment you open your eyes to a new day and realize you are still alive, you are confronted with choices. When adversity strikes and knocks you down, you choose whether you get up or stay down. If you choose not to get up, one thing is certain—your life won't change from where you are. Getting up after falling down gives you another chance to change your or someone else's life for the better. Falling down teaches you humility. Learn to be humble when you stumble as it makes getting back up a little easier.

Practice Gratitude

Give thanks for what you have. Focus on your blessings. Give thanks for your missteps, hiccups, and shortcomings because you still have life. When you live your life with an attitude of gratitude there is always an abundance of blessings and opportunity. You can begin with a practice or daily habit of committing time to focus on that for which you're grateful. Creating a gratitude journal for the sole purpose of capturing gratitude is a great way to build your reservoir of resilience as a tangible reference you can turn to when you need a reminder of how blessed you are.

Power Up Your PMA (Positive Mental Attitude)

Seeing the glass half full helps you to see life on the upswing. Life and the lens you view it through is a matter of perspective. Countless studies support the premise that having a positive mental attitude (PMA) produces a healthier and more stable life existence. When you have a PMA, it helps to build your resilience. When you live with a PMA, you tend to find a silver lining in even the worst of circumstances. It makes adversities easier to bear.

Feeding your mind positive thoughts over negative ones gives you a brighter, more pleasant disposition that can be felt by your presence and attitude in the company of others. I find today that people prefer to shun pollyannaish behavior while internally appreciating or admiring the altruistic optimism it portrays.

Into every life, some rain will fall. When you power your strengths with resilience, you are less inclined to wait for the storm to pass because you are equipped, empowered, and strong enough to dance in the rain and be intentional in your pursuit of leadership success. In the words of an iconic woman, Tina Turner, whose life journey was nothing less than a triumph of resilience, she shared how easy it is to shift to a PMA.

> *"At every moment we always have a choice, even if it feels as if we don't. Sometimes that choice may simply be to think a more positive thought."*
>
> —Tina Turner, American singer and songwriter

"A" Teams for Intentional Leaders

It's good every now and then to reach out to trusted colleagues, mentors, advisors, and friends—people who know you well and will give you an honest perspective on you as a person and a leader. This is kind of like a formal informal reality check. You might think of it like a 360-degree assessment, presenting the same questions to everyone. How you choose to conduct it is up to you, so be honest with yourself about your transparency in using this process. To add a layer of independence to the process, you may want to use a third-party administrator to conduct the 360.

There is value to be gleaned from the critics, naysayers, and adversaries in your life. You might consider adding a few of them to your 360 if that's a course of action you choose to pursue. Independently gaining their perspectives of you is a value add. They help to keep you focused, humble, intentional, and resilient about your purpose as a leader.

DEVELOPING YOUR "A" TEAMS WITH PABs AND PPCs

Your Personal Advisory Board (PAB)

Several years ago, reading an article about leaders of boutique businesses leveraging professional relationships to create personal advisory boards (PABs) captured my curiosity. After doing more research on the subject, it turned out to be a pretty good idea to create a PAB to serve as a sounding board, referral source, team with which to vet ideas, and a supplier of needed expertise. Using your PAB to solicit honest feedback is a powerful element for a leader and business owner of any size.

Here's a comment a member of my PAB shared with me in a note after a major battle as a legislator. It was a win and a loss at the same time. The win was not the popular thing to do, but it was the right thing to do. Her words humbled me and allowed me to understand the commitment and impact of my leadership as a servant leader. She's a trusted colleague, mentor, confidante, and friend who wanted to remain anonymous.

> *"You are an example of learning that life may not be easy or fair, however, as a leader, one must carry on with making the world a better place. You have demonstrated how to admit error, learn, and adapt to frailty and be willing to help others understand the value of all of that. That's grace. That's resilience. That's leadership."*
>
> —PAB Member

YOUR PERSONAL PIT CREW (PPC)

Another group of people to consider as essential to your resilience is what I call your personal pit crew (PPC). These are people close to you who know your inner workings. They know you in a different way than the rest of the world. They have an inside track that addresses the personal side of who you are as a human being. Members of your PPC are the professional practitioners who support your physical, mental, and emotional health and well-being and enable you to do and be the leader you are in service to others.

Learning about yourself, your strengths, and your weaknesses from members of your PPC or some other trusted resource person or group is a tool to build your reservoir of resilience. PABs and PPCs are both components of resilience you may want to add as specific "A" teams. There are things I've learned through the perspectives of others about how resilience provides the fortitude to move forward even when you think you can't. I've shared a couple responses received from members of both these specific "A" teams that are part of my resilience building and practice. Here is what a member of my PPC shared:

> *"Her positive attitude towards everything in her life is truly inspiring. She exudes a resilient spirit of joy through her pain. There's little that I can think of that keeps her from pressing forward in her service to others. During my [twenty] years of providing professional care, Helen has left a deep impression on me and has become a role model for me to learn from."*
>
> —Dr. Sheng Wang, CMD, LAc, Acupuncture Medicine Center

What's significant here about your PAB and PPC members is how they serve to undergird the stability of your foundation. They are core people who support your professional life as a leader, serving to keep you at your best. Having a professional advisory board and a personal pit crew are intentional assets that help you build your reservoir of resilience that supports your health and well-being. These are essential elements that intentional leaders rely on and keep close by.

REFLECTIVE QUESTIONS AND NOTES

What did you do to rebound from your last knockdown? (Be as specific as you can.)

How well equipped are you today for your next leadership challenge?

When the thorns of your life humble you and disrupt your livelihood, what do you do to turn it around?

WELL-BEING

"Caring for myself is not self-indulgent. It is self-preservation."
—Audrey Lorde, American writer, professor, philosopher, poet,
and civil rights activist

I love this quote by Audrey Lorde. The power that lives in those few words encompasses what it means when you're focused on your own self-care as part of your self-preservation. She shared this remark in her book, *A Burst of Light*, published in 1988. She wrote it soon after her second diagnosis of cancer. It came, it went, and it came back again.

Self-care is the combination of wellness and well-being. One without the other really diminishes your power to lead at your best. When you focus on the interconnectedness of wellness and well-being, hopefully, you'll understand the power of these two together to support your role as a vibrant, healthy, and holistic leader.

CHAPTER 11

THE WHOLENESS OF WELL-BEING

"In the pursuit of health and well-being, remember that balance is key. It's not about perfection but about making progress."
—Michelle Obama, former US first lady

I recently attended a learning session for coaches, and the topic was burnout. Burnout is real, and it's not getting better. It's increasing as employee disengagement continues to rise. When you think about what the last couple of years of the COVID-19 pandemic have been like, is it any wonder? It's even more reason to focus on both your wellness and well-being.

It's time for us to be more mindful of how our bodies communicate with us. Our bodies continually give us signs and signals about things that upset the stability of our human ecosystem like stress, burnout, and mental health disorders. We can do better, and our very livelihood relies on our ability to strive for good health and well-being. Beyond eating right and getting sufficient rest, having a healthy work-life balance is crucial, especially if we are to lead others. Wellness and well-being are not the same, and they are both essential elements to your holistic health.

THE DIFFERENCES BETWEEN WELLNESS AND WELL-BEING

What's the difference between wellness and well-being? The dictionary defines *wellness* as "the quality or state of being healthy in body and mind."[1] It primarily addresses the care of your physical being, your body temple. *Well-being*, on the other hand, is defined as, "a state characterized by health, happiness, and prosperity."[2] This is far more expansive than wellness when you think about it. They're not the same, but they are related. Well-being includes wellness. Our focus is on well-being.

Well-being is a holistic practice for continued self-investment across the multiple areas of your life that support and sustain your overall wellness. The practice of well-being is essential to your ability to optimize your leadership growth and development and take your role as a leader to the next level and beyond with intention. Well-being is an iterative process you can use and continue to build upon throughout your leadership tenure and for the rest of your life.

Well-being is also subject to differences that reveal biases—conscious and unconscious—that lead to inequities that impede the path of intentional leadership. One of the more noticeable ways of witnessing or experiencing this difference or discrimination is through the health inequities between men and women. As more leaders become intentional leaders, there is hope that these differences will be mitigated or eliminated sooner than later.

WOMEN LEADERS, WELL-BEING, AND HEALTH INEQUITIES

Sharing as a woman is the context I know and understand best. Overall, I believe women are more attentive to our own wellness, and we tend to have more open discussions about our health and well-being. We get regular annual exams, or at least we're more aware that we should. As women, we tend to pay more attention to the signs and signals, the language our bodies use to communicate with us—the unusual aches and pains, bumps and lumps, and other indicators outside of the norm.

Modern science advancements and the differentiation between women and men of life-robbing conditions have contributed to lifesaving measures for women. The next challenge on the horizon to explore from an equitable and inclusive perspective are the gender, racial, and cultural differences in diagnosis, treatment, and mortality. What may seem insignificant and too subtle in which to invest research dollars and trials to understand and be better informed by one group can be catastrophic to another.

Women have enough challenges to confront as leaders. Wellness and well-being are essential to our success.

The disruptions to work due to childbirth and motherhood are known detractors to leadership opportunities and promotions. As women age and experience the effects of menopause, our leadership can feel derailed by physiological changes beyond our control. It can be an awkward moment when, in the middle of a presentation, you have a visible hot flash in a room dominated by men.

Incidents such as these can potentially impair your physical, emotional, and mental well-being. By choosing to ignore, delay, or subvert addressing your wellness, you may unwittingly derail your leadership prowess. Recognizing and advocating for more equitable and inclusive treatment along your ascent to the boardroom would increase the success factor for many organizations.

If your desire is to be more intentional about your leadership, learning is key to your success. When you choose to build bridges to break down the barriers of division that separate us, you are on your way to improving your well-being.

LIFELONG LEARNING AND WELL-BEING

What I've learned along this journey of leadership is that the most effective leaders are lifelong learners. You make the difference in how the world receives, perceives, and responds to you. When you invest in being your best, nothing's lost, and you become a better version of you.

As a leader, you invest in the people you engage and work with as colleagues, peers, subordinates, customers, and clients. Everyone who comes into your path is impacted by your continual process of learning and growing to be the best leader you can be. When you engage in lifelong learning, it makes a difference and contributes to your well-being. It helps you grow deeper within so your presentation to the world is the culmination and combination of your continual learning and well-being.

For more than twenty years, my youngest sister ran a very successful home-based daycare business. Her business grew by word of mouth and referral. By the time her little angels graduated from full-time daycare, they knew their ABCs and could read and write. This gave her clients—the children and their parents—an advantage of beginning school well-equipped with basics beyond survival. They were prepared to thrive!

In an effort to engage in adult learning and to keep her mind sharp, she began to explore ways to learn during her workday. With some imagination and a change of routine, during the children's naptime, she would engage her laptop and learn new skills whether it was a cooking a new recipe, learning how to fold a shirt in three easy steps, or preparing for a career shift.

Today, my sister is an insurance agent. She closed her daycare business and launched a new career as an empty nester. She transformed her stay-at-home life, raising infants and toddlers, to helping adults take better care of securing their future for loved ones through having life insurance. By the way, she was such a successful daycare provider, that she had a perpetual waitlist for new insurance clients.

She still invests in lifelong learning to keep her senses and professional skills sharp. She now conducts training sessions for new insurance agents and has built a team of agents to expand her business. Her success has afforded her opportunities to travel on the insurance companies' dime to far-away places as a result. She continues to make time to learn new things, personally and professionally. She's taught me a few things as well. That's a pretty good payoff from lifelong learning.

Today, there are countless opportunities and ways to engage in lifelong learning. Sometimes it may even feel like you're bombarded by these ways—emails, pop-up promotional advertising on websites, electronic magazines, periodicals, and news coverage.

Don't discount your own curiosity as an opportunity to expand your body of knowledge and increase your expertise in a particular area. This may include professional and personal interests beyond your current role or responsibilities. It may be the precursor to your next big move. You have nothing to lose and only everything to gain.

There are the educational conferences (in-person and/or virtual), webinars, and professional organization/association offerings. Some may be required by your organization or an upline senior leader to whom you report. If you hold a professional credential(s) that requires continuing professional education credits (CPEs) to maintain it or them, this is a way to stay abreast of changes and remain current in that area. CPEs are another way to indulge your lifelong learning.

Consider continual education like a professional vitamin that's needed for your long-term and sustainable success as a leader. Your well-being is achieved when you have a conscious awareness of the multiple contributing components that allow it to touch all parts of your life. When you embrace the wholeness of well-being is when your leadership opens up to receive the full value of what it means to live as an intentional leader.

REFLECTION QUESTIONS AND NOTES

What is the difference between your wellness and well-being?

How does lifelong learning influence your growth and development as a leader?

Lifelong learning is a powerful tool. What are three ways you can intentionally use lifelong learning as a tool for leadership development and professional growth for the people you lead?

CHAPTER 12

FRAMEWORKS OF WELL-BEING

"Well-being cannot exist just in your own head. Well-being is a combination of feeling good as well as actually having meaning, good relationships and accomplishment."

—Martin Seligman, PhD, American psychologist, educator, and author

It's interesting how major life transitions offer us opportunities to pause or stop and consider a different path to pursue. Winding down twenty-plus years as a local elected official presented for me a host of life changes for consideration. Being the eternal optimist who has always seen the glass half-full versus half-empty led to the study, understanding, and practice of strengths and positive psychology in my work. I continue to believe in the pollyannaish happily ever after life. Well-being is the rubric that makes it possible.

Well-being is not a one-size-fits-all construct. There are multiple theories and variations of frameworks on the subject. Here are a few that have influenced and contributed to the viability of a whole person or a holistic approach to well-being.

I've adopted well-being as an integral pillar of the Intentional Leadership Process System™ offering in working with leaders, teams, and organizations in our practice.

DR. MARTIN E. P. SELIGMAN
WELL-BEING THEORY (WBT) AND THE PERMA MODEL

I stumbled into the study of positive psychology in a coach training and certification program offered by the Coaching and Positive Psychology (CaPP) Institute. The CaPP Institute is an International Coaching Federation-affiliated coaching program anchored in positive psychology and founded by Valorie Burton. She was a student and graduate of the program created and led by Dr. Martin Seligman at the University of Pennsylvania. This was my gateway entry as a coach into deeper understanding, research, and adoption of positive psychology.

The extensive research into the field of positive psychology began with Dr. Seligman. In 1998, during his inauguration as the new incoming president of the American Psychological Association, he sparked this movement in his address. He spoke about a concept of shifting the focus of psychology away from mental illness and pathology to the study of the good and positive in people.

Psychology's premise has traditionally been rooted in how to provide relief for human suffering. Positive psychology presented a different approach to this work by challenging the field to consider an alternative. This out-of-the-box thinking led to research and study that thrives today and continues to become stronger and more relevant than ever.

Seligman, like Don Clifton, the developer of Clifton-Strengths®, rose as a leader in the field of strengths and positive psychology through his beliefs around a more optimistic path of success for people. Society at large had not really been challenged or motivated to consider, let alone pursue, a different construct focused on the wellness and well-being of people in the study and practice of psychology. These two optimists (and unofficial economists) believed a shift towards a redirection on dollars spent to "fix" people would result in better outcomes and cost savings—in economic terms, from microeconomics to macroeconomics, from individual to society at large.

Strengths and positive psychology are both preferred styles for coaching, training, and consulting when developing leaders. Their influence and impact are confirmed through research and interviews conducted with leaders. They are also more commonly used in my professional circles of colleagues and peers.

Here's a brief look at the pillars of PERMA, according to the work of Dr. Seligman:

P – POSITIVE EMOTION

Positive emotion is the linchpin that leads to flourishing in life. It's more inclusive than happiness alone. It emphasizes the importance of experiencing positive emotions of joy, love, hope, pride, interest, compassion, amusement, contentment, and gratitude. Intentionally incorporating more positive emotions into your daily life as a practice or habit can help you erode negative emotions and build your resilience. Positive emotions can be learned, and cultivating them can enhance your overall well-being and contribute to a happier life.

E – ENGAGEMENT

In the words of Seligman, engagement is "being one with the music."[1] To close your eyes and think about what that feels like is a wonderful metaphor for what has been termed in positive psychology as the embodiment of "flow." This revelation was the result of years of research and study by Hungarian-American psychologist Mihaly Csikszentmihalyi.[2] Both Csikszentmihalyi and Seligman saw an incompleteness in psychology's areas of study; as such, they decided to create a focus on happiness, well-being, and positivity. The goal was to create a field focused on well-being and those conditions necessary for humans to thrive and live rewarding lives.[3] The two worked together to further develop what we know today as positive psychology.

Csikszentmihalyi found that when you are at your most creative, productive, and happy place is when you're in a state of flow. It's defined as "a state in which people are so involved in an activity that nothing else seems to matter; the experience is so enjoyable that people will continue to do it, even at great cost, for the sheer sake of doing it."[4] Flow reflects your optimal level of engagement when the perfect combination of challenge and skill or strength intersect.

When your engagement reaches the level of flow, you lose track of time and feel a sense of fulfillment. Engagement is about finding activities aligned with your strengths and passions. Engagement is also a significant aspect of our need for one another. When you deepen your engagement with the people you lead, it increases your flow and moves you into the realm of intentional leadership.

R – RELATIONSHIPS

Social connections and positive relationships in your life in the PERMA+ model are experienced when you feel loved, valued, and supported by the people in your life. How you know yourself is influenced by the people with whom you interact and engage in meaningful relationships ranging from family, friends, partners, colleagues, bosses, mentors, sponsors, neighbors, and your community at large.

Your interaction in these relationships matters to your overall health and wellness. The more positive and uplifting you are in sharing good news and celebrating success builds stronger and healthier relationships. Your enthusiasm and smile in response to life improve your well-being and satisfaction.

M – MEANING

Your search for meaning or sense of belonging is unique to you. We are created as social beings, and our need for value and worth make a difference in the quality of life we live.

When your purpose in life is tethered to something greater than yourself—a higher purpose—you are better prepared to confront adversities. Finding meaning in your life increases your resilience and equips you to better handle significant challenges. Your ability to focus on what really matters to you is enhanced when you have a clearly defined sense of purpose, a genuine "What am I here for?" understanding.

The meaning or purpose that drives your life is unique and different from anyone else's. It may be cultivated by or pursued as a result of your profession, a religious or spiritual belief, or a social or political cause. The meaning of your life may be realized through a non-professional lens like an extracurricular, volunteer, or community activity.

Gallup CliftonStrengths® asks the question, "Do you have the opportunity to do what you do best every day?" When you can honestly respond "yes," you are in a position to definitively name how your work adds value and enriches your life. Gallup reports that, on average, when you get to do what you do best every day, you are "three times as likely to report having an excellent quality of life, and six times as likely to be actively engaged in the work you do."[5] You will experience greater satisfaction in work and life, fewer health challenges, and a life longer lived. The research continues to confirm this.

A – ACCOMPLISHMENTS

What's your reward for goal attainment? A sense of accomplishment! Yes, in PERMA+, achieving goals and experiencing a sense of accomplishment are significant for your well-being. Your accomplishments reflect that place of achievement, mastery, and competence. The fruit of your preparation, planning, perseverance, and pushing forward to lead your team or organization to achieve the goals you set out to accomplish spells success. Dr. Seligman brings to light a distinction that intrinsic or internal goals yield larger gains in well-being over external goals like fame or fortune.

THE PLUS IN PERMA+

It was Seligman's book *Flourish* that introduced the PERMA+ model of well-being, which is also referred to as PERMA+ theory of well-being. It influenced the development of the Wheel of Well-being self-assessment tool used in my Intentional Leadership Process System™. Professor Seligman's PERMA+ model is an interrelated construct of elements that contribute to your overall well-being and life satisfaction.

While everyone's pursuit of happiness may look differently, the PERMA+ model provides a framework for understanding the key components that can lead to a more fulfilling and flourishing life for you. Positive psychology researchers and practitioners often use this model to guide interventions and strategies aimed at enhancing well-being and helping individuals lead happier lives.

Let's take a closer look at Dr. Seligman's PERMA+ model. PERMA has five elements considered the core components of well-being and are designed to help you flourish and lead a meaningful life. They are interrelated, and the more they align with each other in your life, the higher the probability for individuals, teams, organizations, and systems to thrive and flourish together. PERMA+ encapsulates the permanent building blocks of living a profound life as a leader with intention.

The plus in PERMA+ includes other important elements for wholeness or happiness in life. Seligman points to four additional or overlapping elements that are essential to our mental well-being. I know these elements well.

It's interesting when you think about the not-so-subtle shifts in work-life balance brought on because of the pandemic; it is mind-boggling. The initial thought of working from home seemed almost like a staycation except you still had to work. For the first few weeks, it was great to not have to get up at the crack of dawn to prepare for an hour-plus one-way commute to the office.

This was the beginning of new habits that were not in alignment with well-being from a PERMA+ perspective. It was a gradual decline of a relatively healthy work-life balance. The shutdown initiated an encroachment of work overtaking life. Healthy life habits were overcome by workaholism that lasted beyond the pandemic. Going to bed with notes and reminders to prepare for the next day's overcrowded agenda put me on a path to burnout. The world changed and not for the better.

Today, the rise of attention given to our mental health is more important than ever. COVID-19 turned the world upside down, and as we're finding our way to a new "set-point," so to speak, it raises the following to a higher level of attention that increases the viability of PERMA with the +. Optimism, physical activity, nutrition, and sleep represent the + of PERMA+.

OPTIMISM

Optimism is directly associated with positive emotions or the "P" in PERMA+. This is the glass-half-full perspective. When you lead with optimism, there's a higher probability that you will be more resilient when faced with adversities. You'll probably live longer with lower levels of sadness, depression, and clinical mental health challenges.

PHYSICAL ACTIVITY

Physical activity has been recognized as a plus to a happier life by the sheer nature of its physiological effect on good health. Negative emotions like stress, loneliness, burnout, and hopelessness interfere with your good health and contribute to an increased risk of physical and mental health ailments.

For years, AARP has stressed the value of walking thirty minutes a day to improve your physical health, which plays a part in improving your mental health and well-being. Activating your endorphins for a limited amount of time with regularity enhances your happiness and life longevity.

NUTRITION AND SLEEP

Nutrition and sleep seem like no-brainers. However, it takes an intentional focus to have them support your wellness and well-being. Everything you eat is not necessarily nutritious nor does three to four hours of sleep a night constitute being well-rested. The bottom line is we are a complicated species and to live optimally and holistically happy requires conscious and intentional action.

While researching and writing this book, I was convinced to look at my own PERMA+ conditions. As one that used to work all hours of the day and night, needless to say, without a commute during the COVID-19 shutdown, my boundaries of nutrition and sleep went out the window. Nutrition and sleep offered little support for wellness and well-being.

Upon realizing this truth, I made the conscious decision to go to bed no later than midnight even if I didn't feel tired. I found that waking up to a new day, refreshed by a good night's rest, had a profound impact on my ability to get more things done. Oh my goodness. What a difference it makes on a macro and micro level.

PROFESSOR ANTHONY GRANT
WELL-BEING AND ENGAGEMENT FRAMEWORK
(WBEF)

Attending a global webinar for coaches focused on well-being was my introduction to the work of coaching psychologist, Professor Anthony Grant from The University of Sydney.

The webinar referenced some highlights of his work that created enough interest for me to pursue further inquiry into his well-being and engagement framework (WBEF). Via his article, "ROI is a Poor Measure of Coaching Success: Towards a More Holistic Approach Using a Well-being and Engagement Framework,"[6] Grant drew me in to want to know more.

As a CPA and executive leadership coach, here was another compelling reason for me to write this book. Dr. Grant took a hard look at the incompatibility of using financial return on investment (ROI) to measure the success of coaching outcomes.[7] His WBEF opened the opportunity to understand the value of coaching to support leaders and the daily demands and challenges they face in their drive toward success.

The WBEF's origin was in the work Dr. Grant collaborated on with Professor Gordon Spence, a colleague from The University of Sydney. They published a chapter, "Using Coaching and Positive Psychology to Promote a Flourishing Workforce: A Model of Goal-Striving and Mental Health," in the *Oxford Handbook of Positive Psychology and Work* in January 2009. The common threads that tie this work to intentional leadership are positive psychology, the workplace, engagement, and well-being.

The WBEF further refined and supported research resulting in my development of the Wheel of Well-being assessment tool. It was designed to support leaders and teams to self-check their own well-being across the areas identified as essential to achieving optimal success. The connections among strengths, well-being, engagement, and performance are highly correlated to each other. Dr. Grant's framework presents a hard and soft approach for meeting the goals of business to see an ROI while supporting the well-being of the leaders who make it possible.

His work shaped the beginning of a more balanced truth about the hard and soft, tangible and intangible factors used to measure and determine success from a more holistic perspective. Executive coaching and leadership development have become more integral and intentional additions to support the success of leaders, teams, and organizations.

The Two Dimensions of the WBEF

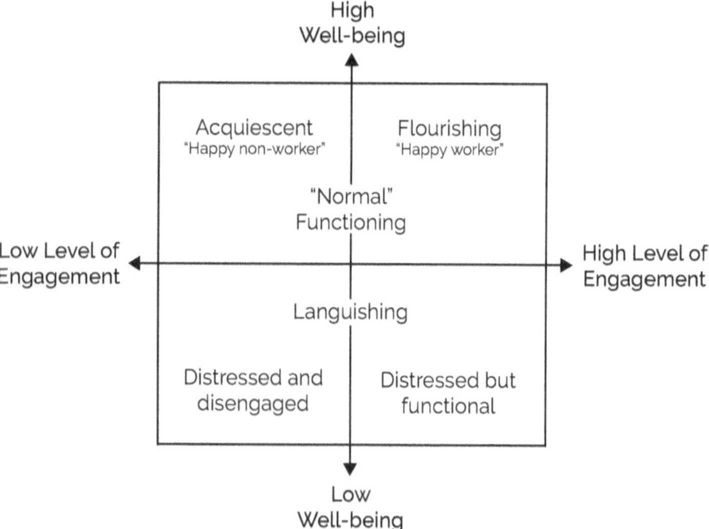

There are two dimensions to the framework. Along the vertical axis is well-being from high to low, and the horizontal axis is focused on workplace engagement from low level to high level.

The area in the upper right quadrant, Flourishing, represents an individual who is actively engaged, self-aware, and operating in high engagement. This reflects an optimal state of well-being. The entire top half of the framework represents "normal functioning."

To the left of "Flourishing" is "Acquiescent," identified as the "happy non-worker," the team member who shows up with positive levels of well-being. This is great for the individual; however, it's not so good for the workplace. As a leader, this is an important indicator for you. These are your team members or employees who are good with their well-being but are not actively engaged in the goals of the workplace.

As you move closer to the horizontal axis, be mindful that it is possible to slip into "Languishing." This is an opportunity for you to be more intentional about the well-being of your team members individually and collectively. The bottom half of the quadrant begins in "Languishing," and this state of being introduces the challenge of well-being slipping into distress and low well-being.

Beneath "Flourishing" is the stronger side of "Languishing." This quadrant resides in the area of having a high level of engagement in the workplace. When your team falls in this area, you are experiencing distress. It may be overlooked because they are still functioning well.

If your team shows up in the lower left quadrant, this is when an intervention is needed. Your team is physically and emotionally languishing in distress, and they are actively disengaged in your workplace. This is the area where your quiet quitters show up, marked by a low level of engagement and low well-being.[8]

Grant's research informed the elusiveness and ineffectiveness of using the financial ROI formula to measure the success of coaching in the workplace—once again, pointing to a correlation of the two important things to compare, financial growth and leadership success through coaching. This version offers an alternative to an ineffective metric that didn't work.

CREATING MY OWN WHEEL OF WELL-BEING

Grant's framework on how to measure well-being in the workplace increased my curiosity in the pursuit of integrating new knowledge and information of relevance in the work on well-being. After studying and reviewing Grant's work, I concluded that strengths, resilience, and well-being are the essential pillars of intentional leadership in the workplace and in life. His research gave validity to how to achieve coaching success in the workplace and benefits that support well-being.

This corroborated much of what I believe and hold true. The big picture focuses on engagement overall and not just in the workplace. Your engagement in life overall matters and makes a difference. Who you are is who you are. Efforts to compartmentalize your life as a leader decrease your well-being in the long run. Here is where your awareness of the interconnectedness of all aspects of your life empowers you as an intentional leader.

As a lifelong learner, spending time exploring, expanding, and challenging relationships among strengths, resilience, well-being, engagement, and performance, I continue to draw attention to correlations among them. Connectedness® is my number one Strength®, and the ideas and theories around these seemingly independent attributes of successful leaders feed an affinity toward holistic well-being for me. I point these out to place an emphasis on the three pillars of intentional leadership (strengths awareness, resilience, and well-being) and the opportunity for you to consider how they correlate with you and your dominant strengths. They must make sense to you before you can make the case for your leadership.

As I have shared the correlation of key factors of leadership and how you can recognize and maintain your own wellness through well-being, it's time to look at how these parts have come together in my concise seven-point methodology to guide you as a leader moving into the realm of intentional leadership. They will help you to lead with wellness in mind, and how to coach and guide your team and organization will follow suit.

REFLECTION QUESTIONS AND NOTES

How will you use your influence as an intentional leader to increase your engagement with your team? With your organization?

____

____

____

____

____

What challenge(s) do you face in identifying your unique meaning, purpose, and fulfillment for your life?

____

____

____

____

____

CHAPTER 13

THE WHEEL OF WELL-BEING

"Holistic well-being is about fostering a sense of connection—
to oneself, to others, and to the world at large."
—Arianna Huffington, co-founder of *The Huffington Post*,
founder of *Thrive Global*, and author

The lens through which life presents itself as an African American woman is shaped by the context of my Black experience in the world. Understanding myself as a leader and considering the challenges faced due to perceptions of race, sex, and culture add a unique and different contribution to the more widely accepted theories and frameworks used in the development of well-being. I believe true well-being is found when your spirit is nourished, your work fulfills you, your relationships uplift you, your body and mind are vibrant, your finances provide stability, and your community thrives in harmony.

My Wheel of Well-being is supported by the wealth of knowledge gained from a diverse community of leaders, researchers, coaches, psychologists, clergy, and professional networks—some of which I shared in previous chapters. Years of research, study, formal education, and work experience led to the development of a framework that captures the perspectives, values, and practices of a non-dominant culture in America.

In other words, the framework inside this chapter is mine. I've developed it to present a platform for intentional leadership through strengths awareness, resilience, and well-being. It has been influenced, reviewed, and supported by the incredible research of other intentional leaders.

The Wheel of Well-being (The Wheel) is an effective self-assessment tool integrated into the Intentional Leadership Process System™ when working with leaders, teams, and organizations. It provides an added measure of monitoring your wellness through well-being to support and sustain the transformation of stronger and more resilient intentional leadership within you and throughout your organization.

Seven interconnected spokes make up the Wheel of Well-being: career well-being, family well-being, social well-being, financial well-being, health well-being, community well-being, and faith/belief well-being. Together, they represent a holistic approach to comprehensively bring a focused awareness and opportunity for you to improve and keep your well-being well-balanced. We use the metaphor of a wheel because it's easier to visualize the ability of a wheel to function and roll smoothly at its best and not so well when it's out of balance.

- What's it like when you realize you have a flat tire as you're riding down the road?
- How does the imbalance of your wheel get your attention?
- What actions do you take to keep your wheel rolling smoothly?

A wheel, once balanced, can easily become unbalanced depending on the circumstances in your life. Periodically reviewing where the spokes of your wheel are out of balance on a scale of one to seven is a helpful exercise. You assess each spoke of the wheel against guidelines of recommended criteria, and your wheel is shaped by your responses. There's no right or wrong way to assess yourself. Your most accurate results are revealed when you are totally honest with yourself. Periodic check-ins can help you identify gaps of imbalance sooner rather than later. As a leader, the more holistically balanced you are in your well-being reduces the possibility of becoming over-extended or experiencing extreme levels of stress, burnout, and disengagement.

When you lead and incorporate the elements of well-being, you are demonstrating concern for yourself and the people you lead. Every time I'm on a flight, before that plane takes off, the flight attendant instructs us that in an emergency, we are to put on our masks first before we attempt to help anyone else. It reminds me of a quote by Maya Angelou who said, "People will forget what you said, people will forget what you did, but people will never forget how you made them feel." The ability to embrace these two thoughts—focusing on yourself first so you are then able help others and remembering the impact you have on them with your action—is a major move toward becoming a more intentional leader.

The Wheel is also a good communication tool to engage in difficult conversations around race, gender, culture, and other areas of diversity less visible than these mentioned. When you understand the more significant elements of culture, attitudes, beliefs, roles, and actions, the parts of who you are that are not visibly seen are experienced through your behavior and ways of being. As was the case with the Titanic, you don't know what's coming at you until there's a collision.

When the vessel hit the massive underwater iceberg, the entire the iceberg was not completely visible to crew. What we see above the water are the objective aspects of culture such as food, clothing, and music. That's not where the most important part of who we are is seen. What lies beneath the water are the more subjective aspects of culture. They are less visible yet create more challenges and opportunities in interactions.

Use The Wheel as a tool or prompt for you to think more deeply about yourself and others with whom you engage who are different from you. The difference in race, gender, age, or some other visible sign can be your opener for a deeper conversation. It builds your capacity for more authentic, open, and transparent conversations that can shed light on how to be more inclusive in the ranks of leadership.

A consciousness of your own understanding of how inclusive you are or are not opens a window of opportunity for you to reflect on your own differences that make you unique, and it presents an opportunity for growth. Consider this a starting point for where your lens of inclusion sharpens and becomes more discerning on how to create a deeper sense of belonging for those who are different from the norm in your current leadership environment. Research and data continue to affirm the value of how a more diverse and inclusive leadership generates greater outcomes and success for teams and organizations.

Let's take a closer look at each of these seven spokes that drives the Wheel of Well-being. Each of them plays a crucial role in your viability and sustainability as a person and as an inclusive leader.

1) **Career Well-being:** Is your career a source of daily enjoyment or fulfillment for you?
2) **Family Well-being:** How intact is your nuclear family?
3) **Social Well-being:** What substantial social relationships do you have that sustain you?
4) **Financial Well-being:** How well do you manage money matters?
5) **Health Well-being:** What is the status of your physical, emotional, and mental abilities to get things done well?
6) **Community Well-being:** How do you feel about the environment in which you live?
7) **Faith/Belief Well-being:** What faith, beliefs, or values keep you connected to life and the world?

Today, your life and leadership are continually challenged by the VUCA (volatility, uncertainty, complexity, and ambiguity) environment we live in that can derail the best of your intentions to lead well. Each of the seven spokes contributes to your success as a leader resolved to be more intentional in your leadership.

As we unpack each of these spokes, pay close attention to how they shed light on and bring awareness to areas of your life that may be impeding your ability to lead at your best. This has been an eye-opener for leaders and teams I've worked with, trained, and coached. The Wheel brings an awareness of where you may be out of balance in your life holistically. It can help you discard practices that no longer serve your greater good as a leader and adopt new ones to create or restore a healthier work-life balance.

CAREER WELL-BEING

Is your career a source of daily enjoyment or fulfillment for you?

Alignment with Purpose. When you have a clear sense of purpose in your vocation, you are more likely to be an intentional leader. Being a well-aligned profession provides you with a stronger sense of direction and fulfillment. This enables you to drive your vision and team with passion and commitment. What does this look like?

In the early years of my chosen profession as an accountant, I believed I had a clear sense of purpose. Plans were set to pass the CPA exam and launch a productive career. Within the first few years of practicing my chosen profession, it became clear that having a natural knack for numbers was not enough to fulfill me.

Placing blame on things outside of me increased the disconnect between purpose and fulfillment. Losing perspective on your alignment with your purpose has repercussions that can lead to burnout, lack of motivation, and a disconnect from active engagement to being actively disengaged from your role, vision, and goals.

Making the time for regular self-assessment and career realignment is a way to circumvent these pitfalls. As a leader, when you neglect your own sense of purpose, you may struggle to effectively lead, inspire, and guide your team. It took me years of hit-or-miss attempts to find the right path of restoration and realignment.

Having the necessary talent, skills, and abilities to be a fit for your career doesn't necessarily mean it provides joy and fulfillment. It takes courage to step away from what you can do to pursue what you want to do that brings you joy. Leaders who bridge the gap do so with an attitude of intention that propels them to move into the realm of intentional leadership.

Aligning your career with a clear sense of purpose leads to a state of well-being that keeps you anchored and growing as an intentional leader. I transitioned from public accounting to public service and aligned my career with purpose, passion, and professional fulfillment.

FAMILY WELL-BEING

How intact is your nuclear family?

Support System. A strong family foundation provides emotional support and stability. An intentional leader draws strength from their family, helping them navigate challenges in their professional life with a balanced and holistic perspective and with resilience. Your nuclear family is a crucial support system that contributes to your emotional well-being.

Who is your nuclear family? It's important to clarify what a nuclear family may look like today. Growing up in the 1960s, a nuclear family was considered two parents consisting of a mother and father and their children living in a single household. The typical family structure included biological and/or adopted children and was distinct from extended family. In the Black community, though, it was not uncommon for the nuclear family to include grandparents, aunts, uncles, or cousins living together or being closely involved in your nuclear family's life.

I grew up in a single-parent family in the 1960s as the result of divorce that occurred when I was around the age of six. It made me stand out from most of my peers. And now, as a single adult without children, my construct of family has never aligned with more traditional structures like the two-parent model.

Today, the concept of a nuclear family is flexible, adaptable, and creative, representing the diversity and inclusion of family life as we each personally choose it to be. Although our world still grapples with how to fully embrace inclusion, modern day families reveal more inclusive families than ever before.

The diversity of families exists today in the multiple configurations we see ranging from racially mixed and same-sex marriages, to blended families by divorce, to adoptions of children from different races and nationalities. These family structures represent inclusion by way of diversity. Research and countless studies continue to monitor and report on the positive impact of inclusion through diversity on leaders, teams, and organizations when embraced.

My current nuclear family is a chosen family comprised of what remains of my nuclear family from my childhood along with friends and colleagues who share a deep and emotional bond and commitment to supporting each other like that of a traditional family. A strong family foundation contributes to your well-being, offering stability and balance that enables you to navigate the challenges of leadership more holistically grounded.

When you, as a leader, fail to prioritize your well-being, it can put a strain on your family relationships and damage family bonds. This can work two ways in that your family can also be the source of disruption to your well-being. Setting boundaries and prioritizing quality time with family will help you avoid the pitfalls of leadership that come at the expense of personal connections. It encourages you to recognize the interdependence of professional and personal success.

SOCIAL WELL-BEING

What substantial social relationships do you have that sustain you?

Networking and Relationship Building. Intentional leaders know the importance of social connections and how to leverage their networks for success. The art of networking and relationship building is showcased by intentional leaders who have harnessed the power of social connections to gain insights, foster collaboration, and drive their visions forward.

The social side of well-being is anchored in building bridges to break down barriers to your success.

The cost of minimizing or neglecting your networks as a leader may cause you to become a leader who serves in isolation. We are created as relational beings, and isolation-ism is not how intentional leaders lead. The implications of ignoring or being unaware of the importance of social con-nections can cause you to miss out on valuable insights and collaboration opportunities. Intentional networking and relationship-building are significant to your ability to be a successful leader. The consequences of being disconnected from your industry and peers is too high a cost to pay and is not an effective way of supporting your well-being.

As an elected official, social relationships and connections were essential parts of my ability to get things done. It became evident as I transitioned from that role to the next as the exec-utive director of a national nonprofit organization. It involved years of cultivating strong relationships locally and globally. The ability to pick up a phone and solicit the support of another leader on the strength of a relationship is what elevates ordinary leaders to intentional leaders who understand the value of social well-being. It's a professional stress reducer.

FINANCIAL WELL-BEING

How well do you manage your money matters?

Stability and Freedom. Financial well-being provides leaders with the stability and freedom to make strategic decisions without being solely driven by financial concerns. Intentional leaders focus on long-term goals and investments, fostering sustainable success.

When a leader is unsuccessful in managing their financial well-being, there are repercussions that manifest. Poor financial decisions and lack of strategic planning can lead to organizational instability and financial crises, professionally and personally. The importance of financial literacy is significant for leaders. The neglect of this aspect can compromise the long-term success of both the leader and the organization. It is not a healthy position for an intentional leader.

There was a time in life when I didn't manage money well at all. Then, one day, I found myself absorbed in a workshop about managing your finances. The truth is many of us spend up to the level of what we have coming in and sometimes beyond. I got hooked on credit cards right out of college. It seemed so easy to manage them with a full-time career, earning a salary versus working an hourly job for a paycheck. This was a hard lesson learned that took years to repair.

As you prepare for retirement or semi-retirement, now is the time to determine how and what you will live on to live comfortably. Whatever the case may be, don't wait until the time comes to begin to figure it out. You can't always predict if or when you will find yourself in a position where you are not working or where you are unable to work to earn an income, but you can be proactive and plan for the moment. It can be frightening and painful to find yourself in a predicament that could have been minimized or avoided.

Put away a portion of every dollar you earn or receive to support a smoother transition when the unexpected occurs. Whether it's that rainy day you hoped you'd never see or the early retirement you hadn't planned for, the landing is a little better with a level of cash reserves above zero. The standard recommendation has been to have three to six months of regular living expenses on hand, and you may want to include the extras you indulge in when there's no threat on the horizon.

Today, the goal is closer to needing to have a year's worth of essential expenses available as liquid assets that are easily accessible. This doesn't rule out investments like real estate, precious metals and gems, or other appreciable assets. The difference is that when you're faced with a burden that doesn't necessarily afford you the time for quick liquidation, cash reserves can help bridge the gap.

Then, there are the anticipated expenses like college tuition for your children, professional development or highly skilled training or education for yourself, or maybe it's the dream vacation on your bucket list. Here is where a savings plan helps to ease the burden to meet the need if and when it arrives. It's so much nicer to take a bucket list vacation and, when departure time arrives, know it's paid for in full, including spending money in your pocket.

HEALTH WELL-BEING

What is the state of your physical and mental health to get things done well?

Energy and Resilience. Physical and mental wellness directly impacts your leadership effectiveness. The connection among your health, energy level, resilience, and decision-making abilities are intertwined. Intentional leaders put practical strategies in place to prioritize their health well-being that supports their ability to lead with vitality.

When you neglect your physical and mental health, the consequences that follow show up as stress, poor lifestyle choices, or burnout that can significantly impact your leadership effectiveness. I cannot stress enough the importance of prioritizing your health holistically as a way to sustain your leadership. You must become the chief advocate, as the leader, to create a culture that values health and well-being as a cornerstone of leadership excellence. That's a laudable goal to model for those you lead that has the benefits of improved health, lower absenteeism, and positive cost savings.

Twenty years ago, I was four to five dress sizes larger than I am today. In 1996, as a freshly minted city councilwoman, I wasn't aware of how much food and beverage was shared in community meetings; receptions; celebrations; ribbon-cuttings; galas; breakfast, lunch, and dinner meetings. It was considered rude not to accept the hospitality extended to elected representatives.

Being the foodie that I am, within a few short years, forty pounds piled onto my petite five-foot-three-inch frame. How did that happen? When have you asked yourself a similar question in the aftermath of not being fully present to the changes happening in your life? Having been a yo-yo dieter, my weight going up and down was not something I wanted to do ever again.

So, what did I do? I bought clothes that fit. Somewhere I read that when you wear clothes that fit you, it's less noticeable that you've gained weight. My wardrobe had sizes ranging from six to sixteen. "Oh well. Such is life" is what I told myself until… My primary care physician recommended hypertension medication, and that's when the alarm went off. Your health is the greatest wealth you have, and without it, all your hopes, dreams, and aspirations are at risk.

I joined Weight Watchers to learn how to modify my relationship with food and exercise to improve my health. I vowed years ago to never diet again. Learning sustainable lifestyle modifications allowed me to lose forty pounds and keep it off for more than twenty years and counting.

Health is the area of life that has challenged me the most. Entering a season of life where the demand for more and better self-care in order to function better can be a difficult pill to swallow for a busy leader who's laser-focused on serving others. Learning the value of a good night's rest can be disruptive to your flow of getting things done when you're a driven leader with a full plate. The thought of creating boundaries and structures to support the physiological urges your body is craving and demanding, like sleep, is a challenge that must be addressed.

COMMUNITY WELL-BEING

How do you leverage your leadership to add value to your community?

Social Responsibility. How do you feel about where you live? Is the neighborhood where you live or work changing? What do you do to add value to enrich your community? These questions are all part of your community well-being. It's not just applicable to where you live; it includes where you work as well. When you engage with your community, it fosters a positive reputation and a sense of social responsibility. Intentional leaders understand the importance of contributing to the greater good while enhancing their organization's reputation and creating a positive work environment.

When a leader fails to engage with the community to which they belong, professionally and personally, they may face reputational risks. It could create a disconnect with your social and community-conscious employees, customers, and neighbors. Your missed opportunities to engage could cost your reputation more harm than good over the long term. A prolonged history of disengagement may not be as easy to resuscitate or repair as you might think. As a leader, when you understand the benefits of investing in social responsibility, you're also fostering a culture of collaboration and goodwill, which is a great way to build on your legacy as a leader.

Having served for decades in volunteer leadership positions on boards, commissions, and committees locally and nationally, I've created strong relationships and connections to leverage. It has generated goodwill and opportunities to impact my local community. This can be a pathway for you and those you lead to increase your level of community engagement for your workplace and the community where you live. Consider the multiplicative impact that your actions can have to inspire and improve the well-being of others. It's a great way to initiate and expand community engagement through individual and collective service interests.

SPIRITUAL WELL-BEING

How does your faith, beliefs, or values keep you connected to life and the world?

Faith, Values, and Guiding Principles. Leaders with a strong sense of faith or belief systems often incorporate them into a set of guiding principles by which they live and lead. These principles shape your decision-making and leadership style while providing a moral compass that aligns with your vision and values. The hundreds of interviews and coaching sessions I conducted with leaders of various faith and belief backgrounds shed light on the role of values in intentional leadership.

Most of the models on well-being I've studied don't include faith, belief, or spiritual well-being as a separate element of well-being. However, what you believe about creation and life is significant for most leaders I've encountered. I remember asking Jim Harter, Gallup chairman and co-author of *Well-being at Work*, during a live webinar, "Where does faith or spirituality fit in Gallup's research on well-being?" I was glad he had a plausible response. He replied that spirituality is included in them all. It was a quick save but not in a way that would lead readers and followers to understand or recognize the inclusion of it. Spirituality is not explicitly named, spoken, or referenced in their research.

The whole is greater than the sum of its parts. This is a math theorem I learned in junior high school. Over the years, it continues to surface and ring true in many areas of life. We are complex creations of many parts that are simultaneously moving. Your well-being is wrapped up in you as a whole person impacted by each of the spokes on the wheel as discussed. The Wheel of Well-being is the culmination of internal and external influences that affect your role as a leader, especially an intentional leader.

When a leader neglects their faith or guiding principles, it can erode trust both within your organization and with external stakeholders. There is a need for you, as a leader, to stay true to your beliefs and values. To deviate from your guiding principles can put you at risk for potential fallout of the good work you have done. This element of well-being could collapse the foundation of your reputation if not safeguarded and kept intact.

It's important to understand the individual elements of the Wheel of Well-being because the greatest strength of the Wheel is the interdependence that exists within each spoke. The tool I developed is an assessment that allows you to self-monitor the state of your overall well-being. Once you've taken the assessment for the first time, you then have a starting point to help you be more intentional about leading a holistically balanced life as a leader.

Consider this your invitation to take the Wheel of Well-being assessment. Visit my website, **drhelenholton.com**, to get started, then engage with a Dr. Helen Holton and Associates leadership coach to unpack and discuss the results of your assessment. Give this gift to yourself at least once a quarter to help you remain focused and holistically balanced as an intentional leader.

REFLECTION QUESTIONS AND NOTES

When do you consciously stop to measure your progress toward the achievement of a goal?

How do you intentionally make room for boundaries, rest, and life reflection?

What is your definition of living a balanced life as an intentional leader?

THE ROLE AND PURPOSE OF COACHING WITH INTENTION

CHAPTER 14

WHO ARE THE UNICORNS ON YOUR TEAM?

"In order to be irreplaceable, one must always be different."
—Coco Chanel, French fashion designer and businesswoman

Being in touch with yourself—your true self—is enlightening and empowering. And sometimes, it can be a revelation of how others see you in ways you don't. When you know and can name your uniqueness, it simplifies life and makes it easier to be your most authentic self.

For example, people have said to me, "You're a unicorn." What is a unicorn? How do you get here? Initially rejecting the notion of the comparison to a unicorn led me to look closer at what it meant. After researching what it meant to be recognized as a unicorn, along with some serious introspective work, I understood just how much it described me in a single word. It speaks to the woman I've become and how distinctively different I am from anyone else in a peculiar way reflected in how I show up and do the work I do.

I am a unicorn.

An exceptional individual with a rare blend of educational pursuits; leadership experiences; and earned expertise in government, business, nonprofit, education, and faith sectors. Here's what that looks like through the lens of my life as a committed advocate and ally for inclusion, diversity, equity, justice, belonging, and culture or intercultural competency.

Living life at the intersections of race, gender, political power, and privilege are driving forces that have shaped what leadership looks like. The rooms I've been in, the tables I've had a seat at, and the opportunities to voice a unique perspective to deepen and shift conversations are nothing short of amazing.

Elected to the Baltimore City Council in 1995 as a first-time candidate in a sea of nineteen people running for one of three seats to represent the Fifth District was a unicorn moment. My campaign disrupted the status quo. It was unusual, almost unprecedented, for a single candidate to break a ticket of three candidates running together. This framework ultimately led to a ballot referendum initiative that prevailed and changed the electoral process for people seeking to serve as city council representatives.

I had a strong interest and foundation in government and public policy built over twenty-five plus years of active engagement and investment as a student, concerned citizen, and advocate for fair and effective leadership. These interconnections of life experiences that contributed to my actions started in Mrs. Mazer's sixth grade social studies class. She taught us that the government was created by the people and for the people and that the power of our democracy rested in the will and acts of the people. It was a significant teachable moment early in life that shaped and impacted my life as a leader—a servant leader who leads with intention.

The journey began as a teenager, volunteering on election campaigns for candidates seeking office and supporting causes of interest. College introduced a broader selection of organizations to connect and build capacity with other like-minded people to make a difference. This was my foray into a life of leadership that was not on my radar at the time. Finding my views, perspectives, and voice continued to grow and develop—the beauty of lifelong learning and curiosity as a unicorn.

QUALITIES OF A UNICORN LEADER

I'm not the only unicorn out there, and as a leader, you'll want to know how to spot them for yourself. They could already exist within your team or organization. You, too, could be a unicorn and not even realize it. Yet.

Here's what I've learned about unicorns. The reference to a leader as a "unicorn" is a metaphorical way of expressing that the leader is exceptionally rare and possesses a unique set of qualities or skills. In the context of leadership, calling someone a unicorn suggests that they stand out from the norm. They tend to exhibit extraordinary traits that make them highly valuable and distinctive.

Unicorns have a distinctive uniqueness that's rare and exceptional in a positive way. The vibe you put out into the world resonates on a uniquely different frequency. The combination of your strengths, skills, experiences, and environments produces accomplishments rarely found in another single individual. The scope is wide and the purpose narrow. Unicorn leaders are exceptional individuals who are visionaries, innovators, and catalysts for change. You experience them in all sectors and industries. They are mavericks and change-makers unafraid to take risks.

Let's explore some of the characteristics or qualities that unicorn leaders display.

Innovative Visionary Leadership

They have a clear and compelling vision for the future. Their creative, out-of-the-box, and innovative thinking makes it easy for them to inspire others to follow and believe in their direction. They're able to effectively create a strong sense of purpose for their team and organization.

Exceptional Communication

Effective communication is a hallmark of unicorn leaders. They can clearly and persuasively convey their ideas, visions, and expectations. This is useful in fostering understanding and alignment among team members, stakeholders, and the broader community.

Empathy and Emotional Intelligence

Unicorn leaders demonstrate high levels of emotional intelligence and empathy. They understand the emotions and needs of their team members, which contributes to creating a positive and supportive work environment. This is an essential skill to help build strong relationships and foster collaboration throughout the team and organization.

Risk-Taking

Unicorns are not afraid to take calculated risks. They understand that innovation and progress often involve stepping out of their comfort zone. Their willingness to embrace risk sets them apart and opens opportunities for transformative change.

Resilience

Resilience is an anchor for unicorn leaders. They learn to fail forward and bounce back from setbacks, detours, and interruptions, using them as opportunities for growth. Their resilience enables them to persevere through difficulties and maintain an optimistic outlook.

Impact

Unicorn leaders make a lasting and significant impact on their teams, organizations, industries, and society at large. The contributions they make go above and beyond the norm. They leave a legacy that continues to influence and inspire others.

These are some of the qualities and characteristics that collectively contribute to the unique and exceptional nature of unicorn leaders. They emerge in various fields, including business, technology, politics/social change, education, non-profit, and entertainment sectors. Individuals like Steve Jobs, co-founder of Apple Inc.; Oprah Winfrey, media mogul and philanthropist; Malala Yousafzai, education activist; and Nelson Mandela, former president of South Africa are all considered unicorn leaders.

Unicorn leaders each stand out for the rare, influential, and extraordinary people they are in their respective fields. They contribute to the best of who we are as significant contributors toward the betterment of society. Unicorn leaders are all around us. All you have to do is look for them with a more informed lens of what to look for.

GROOMING THE UNICORNS ON YOUR TEAM

Who are the emerging unicorns on your team? How do you recognize them? Grooming your budding unicorns, or high-potential up-and-comers, on your team is serious business. It begins with you fine-tuning your antenna to see, hear, and experience them. Although they are unique and different, they are worth the investment of your time and effort.

Here are a few ways you, as the leader, can engage a strategic and nurturing approach to support your development of the emerging unicorns on your team:

Identify Potential and Invest in It

It's important for you to regularly assess the performance, skills, and potential of your team members. You want to pay close attention to those who consistently go above and beyond their responsibilities. You invest in the potential of your emerging unicorns with professional development. Provide access to training, workshops, and educational resources that align with their career aspirations.

It's also a good time to consider investing in leadership development training to enhance their managerial and leadership skills. Cultivating leadership skills includes communication, decision-making, and conflict resolution. Your recognized and affirmed emerging unicorns would be good quality candidates for the Intentional Leadership Process System™.

Provide Challenging, Creative, and Cross-Functional Exposure

Offer stretch assignments or challenging projects that allow your emerging unicorn to showcase their skills and take on new responsibilities. Encourage them to exercise creativity and innovative thinking. Give them the freedom to propose and implement new ideas.

If your organization is large enough, you may want to consider cross-training opportunities for exposure to different departments or functions within the team or organization. This broadens their skill set and perspective while preparing them for leadership roles. These opportunities help them to stretch, develop, and demonstrate their capabilities.

Extend Mentorship, Leadership Coaching, and Networking Opportunities

There is room for all three of these simultaneously and separately. Mentors provide guidance, insights, and a supportive environment while they help point the way toward the next correct positions on your unicorn's compass. Having a mentor is typically a long-term relationship and usually with a senior-level person in your organization. It can be with a leader outside your organization; however, you would want them to be in your industry with deep knowledge of your organization. Mentorships are usually non-paid voluntary relationships and tend to require the mentee to take the lead and reach out for regular communication, guidance, and support.

A leadership coach is a subject matter expert who engages with you to support the leadership growth and development of your emerging unicorn. Their goal is to guide the development of strengths and support the coachee in finding their leadership style. Using assessment tools helps your potential unicorns better understand themselves from multiple perspectives.

The role of the coach is to create a safe and trusted environment for the coachee to go deep within to embrace, consciously claim, and leverage who they are at their best. It's a way that helps them hone their knowledge, skills, and abilities to optimize their potential for upward mobility and greater success as an emerging leader. This is the space and place where your unicorn can explore their weaknesses with a coach and develop ways to navigate around them by learning to lean into their strengths.

Professional networking opportunities present an atmosphere to practice the learning and insights gained from a mentor coach. Encouraging participation in industry events and conferences and building a professional network enhances their visibility and opens doors for new possibilities inside and outside of your organization.

These are a few ways to spark your thinking about how to effectively develop and groom your emerging unicorns on the rise. Combining these strategies and incorporating others unique to your organization or industry support their growth and development and ensure their sustained success within your team and organization. The ultimate goal is to strategically nurture the unique qualities of your emerging unicorns and help them evolve into impactful and intentional leaders in their own right.

ACKNOWLEDGING THE UNICORNS YOU LEAD

Referring to a leader as a unicorn is a metaphorical way of expressing that the leader is exceptionally rare and possesses a unique set of qualities and skills. Calling someone a unicorn suggests that they stand out from the norm, exhibiting extraordinary traits that make them highly valuable and distinctive to your team.

Recognizing unicorns within your team or organization involves keen observation and an understanding of the qualities that set exceptional rising leaders apart. As the leader, it's important for you to foster an environment that encourages open communication and feedback—regular check-ins, performance reviews, and team discussions—to glean insights into the strengths and potential of your unicorns.

Supporting and grooming your emerging unicorns involve a strategic and nurturing approach. When you create a supportive environment, it also helps to ensure their success within the organization. Nurturing the unique qualities of your unicorns will help them evolve into impactful and intentional leaders in their own right.

How do you recognize potential leaders on your team that may be unicorns?

____

____

____

____

What unique strengths and skills do you see in the rising leaders on your team?

____

____

____

____

How can you create an inclusive and supportive atmosphere for your leaders to thrive?

____

____

____

____

CHAPTER 15

THE POWER AND VALUE OF COACHING

"A coach is someone who tells you what you don't want to hear, who has you see what you don't want to see, so you can be who you have always known you could be."
—Tom Landry, American professional football coach and player and World War II veteran

In the spring of 2010, one of my closest and dearest friends, Cathy, introduced me to a new business opportunity. It was group coaching for women with a multi-level marketing network format; the coaching was designed to help women get unstuck, face their fears, and grow. Not knowing much about what coaching entailed, I was all ears and excited about a new and different entrepreneurial opportunity.

It was my first formal introduction into the world of coaching. What I didn't know at the time was that it would lead to the passion, purpose, and calling for my life. Becoming a certified coach with Compass Life and Business Designs, which was created to help women transform their lives, was like no other venture I'd encountered before.

The difference this time is that stepping into coaching shifted the direction of my life for the better forever. It was a two-way opportunity—to help others grow and become more while developing myself at the same time was powerful. Unfortunately, Compass didn't survive, but the call to coaching continued to incubate and cultivate a new career path with unlimited potential ahead—an unimagined future forward.

Now was the time for some serious transformative reflection. Was my current position enough to fulfill me beyond a paycheck and other perks? Would the long-term future ahead bring more joy to living? Sometimes you can make a role fit until you look in the mirror and see a different truth.

Leading a team or organization and doing good work doesn't always mean it's your best work. It was time to analyze and assess options for moving ahead and in what direction. These questions took up residence in my mind and challenged me to align what I was doing to what I really wanted to do with my life vocationally. They were strong coaching questions that caused me to seriously consider my day-to-day activity on a deeper level and to assess if I was moving in alignment with my dreams.

As individual human beings, we each live with the same amount of finite time—twenty-four hours a day, seven days a week. They add up to the months and years that mark the time of what we do to become who we are. Time often feels like it's passing by too quickly even though it moves at the same pace for us all. Youth is the elusive elixir that makes you think you have all the time in the world to figure out what you want and how to go after it. However, your dreams never stand a chance if you don't pursue them with a good measure of intentionality.

As you live longer, hopefully, you learn that what you could do in your youth is different when you add a few decades or so. To believe you can deliver with the vigor you did when you were twenty-two is a delusion for most of us. Here's a hard truth beyond denial—we grow old only in our bodies while our minds hold onto our youthfulness of days gone by. Hopefully, your mind catches up with your body. I've reached that place in life. So, now what?

Then, you write a book to tell your story with the hope that it will touch the reader in some profound way to continue your pursuit of purpose, passion, and calling with intention. Why? Because the world needs more intentional leaders like you who know and understand the value of your strengths, the role of a reservoir of resilience, and what it takes to live in a holistic state of well-being.

> *...the most effective leaders are lifelong learners, and whom you learn from matters.*
>
> —Dr. Helen Holton

It began for me by being totally captivated by coaching. That led to formal training, education, and lived practical experience, resulting in earned expertise. What I learned along the way is that the most effective leaders are lifelong learners, and whom you learn from matters. Lifelong learners never reach the finish line. Your commitment to learning is a continual process that keeps you sharp, steady, and striving for excellence in everything you do. It helps you become a more agile learner and intentional leader with flexibility and preparedness to shift, pivot, bob, and weave to keep moving forward—to keep making a difference through your strengths, resilience, and well-being.

When you know yourself better, your impact as a leader is better. As an intentional leader, you recognize the contributing factors to your success. When you know what you're good at and how to navigate your shortcomings or weaknesses, it puts you at an advantage. When you invest in building your most dominant talents into strengths, your performance as a leader is improved exponentially.

John Maxwell, one of my mentors, says "Everything rises and falls on leadership. The world will be a better place when people become better leaders." This fundamental axiom is one of the guiding principles for the work I do. As an intentional servant leader, this is my purpose, passion, and calling—to guide leaders to become intentional leaders.

GOING DEEPER WITH A COACH

I strongly believe in the power of coaching to open and create space for you to go deeper within to uncover, discover, and tap into the you that only you know. Your greatest potential for success as a leader is already within you. This book is your primer to launch your journey forward.

One of my coaches, Coach Louis, referenced the book *What to Say When You Talk to Yourself* by Shad Helmstetter, PhD.

He recommended I get the book audibly instead of in print. (It seems the luxury of sitting and reading a book in hand is rapidly becoming a lost art, often relegated to an activity done only while on vacation. Leaders are busier than ever, moving around the world on planes, trains, and automobiles—wonderful places and spaces to learn and absorb by simultaneously listening to an audiobook or reading an eBook. I've found it a wonderful way to constructively pass the time with an added bonus of gaining information and knowledge to support my intent to better serve my clients.) Listening to my trusted coach made a difference in my willingness and ability to interrupt the negative thoughts of my inner critic. His coaching guided an exploration into deeply rooted negative roadblocks I'd grown comfortable accepting as truths. We all live with an inner critic or two—maybe more. Your inner critic or saboteur often shows up subconsciously first to attack, then to tear you down without conscious concurrence.

Coaching is a practice and process that is effective at revealing your conscious and unconscious derailers of your dreams. Coaching has the potential to bring you to a conscious realization of how you can achieve greater success. It can be a painful and powerful awareness that prompts you to choose whether to invest in becoming a more intentional leader or staying the course in a fuzzy reality you cannot clearly see. We don't know what we don't know, and once you *do* know, it's an opportunity to grow and do better.

Stepping into your hopes and dreams and opening up in ways you may have never considered or dared can be daunting. When you make the time to identify a good coach for yourself, look for someone whose primary interest is you; that's a good place to begin. What makes the difference is their ability to hold you accountable for what you say you want for your life.

Doing deep self-work can be scary sometimes. Your coach's responsibility is to create a safe and trusted environment for the two—coach and client—to work together. This can be in-person, virtually, or a combination of the two. Working with various coaches throughout life for professional development and personal growth is an essential element of my success. It taught me that whenever you find yourself stuck or dissatisfied with a lack of progress, it's time to seek out a professional coach.

There are many kinds of coaches, and it's a worthwhile investment of your time to find a coach whose energy and expertise align with what you want and need. Your coach's primary role is to support you, to hold you accountable to explore and develop your goals and forward action priorities. The courageous conversations you have with your coach that take you outside of your comfort zone are the driving force that fuels your coaching journey. By no means is coaching a quick fix. It takes time, trust, and a stick-to-it-iveness tenacious spirit to achieve your desired outcomes.

As you experience the stories shared here through your own life filters, the hope is that they will motivate and inspire you to want to learn more about who you really are versus who you think you are. This requires a healthy dose of curiosity, courage, and confidence. When you choose to do the work to be a better leader, you tend to produce better results when you work with someone. That someone is preferably a professionally trained and credentialed coach.

As an executive leadership coach, I often use stories for deeper engagement and an emotional connection. When you, as the reader or listener, connect emotionally with a story, you're more likely to remember and better relate to the underlying message. Storytelling is a rich and powerful tool that brings clarity and improved memory retention. Consider the power of the following story and the value of coaching for this leader.

VALUE OF COACHING THROUGH STRENGTHS

Coaching is a pathway to transformation. It's a process that can bring your deepest dreams and desires to life. Martina, a client, reached out in search of a mentor coach while she was in pursuit of her professional coaching credential with the International Coaching Federation (ICF). The time she took to consider coaches and determine the right one for her needs was impressive. Relationships matter. It's a heart-to-head connection for me. It's important for you to get to know the person you're entrusting to help move you forward as your coach.

This matters when you want to be seen, heard, and supported to meet your goals. It's an essential element for a successful coaching relationship—a highly held value of the profession. Every coach is not for every person; however, every person can benefit from a good coach—an important truth to keep in mind.

When we met, Martina was a director in people development with her employer, a multinational global corporation. She enjoyed her role and shared aspirations to move to higher levels. Her organization was supportive in her quest for professional development to become a trained and credentialed coach in her role. Our first meeting was the opportunity to begin building our relationship as client and coach.

It's here that Martina opened up and began sharing her "why" beyond her professional role. This had already been established during the vetting process. This "why" was important because it reached deeper into the heart of what was driving her beyond the job—not to diminish the significance of her career but to take it to the level of personal growth for her life as well.

Listening intently, I heard her passion for being a catalyst to move the needle of diversity, equity, and inclusion (DE&I) forward under her responsibilities as a leader in people development. With more than thirty years of experience in her industry, she believed she was ready for the next level of leadership, and coaching would help her achieve it.

As a first-generation college student and graduate in her family, Martina was used to confronting and overcoming obstacles in pursuit of her dreams. She is a trailblazer for others in her family; she modeled what was possible. Her sights were set high to rise to the global level of leadership in DE&I. Investments in her own personal and professional development earned her vertical and horizontal growth in her industry.

Was this the right time? As we engaged in conversations about opportunities to move ahead, I began to hear her hesitation about moving forward. The subtle excuses and rising roadblocks were creeping in and hoping to gain ground. Her words didn't match up with the vision she'd previously expressed.

As Martina's coach, this was a signal to be more curious and to ask more challenging questions to uncover what was stopping her. What was blocking her forward movement? Your coach brings value to the coaching relationship by creating a safe space for you to go deeper into more probing and courageous conversations.

Think of an infant in his/her mother's womb, warm, protected, and loved. That's the kind of safe space a professional coach seeks to provide—a comforting environment where courageous conversations take place, inviting you to take a deeper look within yourself, a more honest look at your truths, beliefs, and desires.

You know the best answers for your life better than anyone else. They may not always get you the results you're after, however, they will always teach you something. Besides, if you choose to follow someone else's decision about your life, what right do you have to look to blame them when the outcome isn't what you wanted? You are the captain of your ship, the master of your destiny.

Asking you powerful questions designed to help you absorb and process before you go to your automatic response of avoidance or deflection is what a coach does. Their focus is to create a safe environment for you to be vulnerable and go deep to find your best path to get unstuck, remove roadblocks, and keep pressing forward to your goals.

Have you ever tried your hand at gardening? Any potted plants? Flower beds? Vegetable gardens? It took me multiple attempts over the course of a decade or two and new learning to become a decent novice gardener. The point is that coaching takes time. It's not a quick fix to challenges that were probably deeply buried in your subconscious before you ever knew they were there. That's okay. You're here now, and I want to help you gain perspective on the value of coaching.

Over the course of our coaching relationship, Martina had a couple of opportunities to move ahead toward her goal. Hesitation had her stalled, and she went after lower-hanging fruit to placate her true desire. The interview revealed that her heart wasn't fully present for the opportunity, and she didn't land the position. Our coaching relationship upshifted to go deeper with more challenging questions and sessions consisting of brainstorming possibilities. We processed the deeper messages in her objections. She accepted accountability for the introspective work she was challenged to do. This indicated to me that she was ready to move ahead.

Today, Martina is the global head of DE&I for her organization. After the completion of coaching engagements, I stay in touch with my clients, and I reached out to catch up with Martina. I could hear the joy in her voice as she informed me "I've only got a few minutes, Dr. Helen. So good to hear from you."

I was honored she took my call. As she was talking at a rapid pace, she shared that she was preparing to give a global presentation in Switzerland to more than seventy world leaders. Our conversation affirmed for her again the work she did to land her dream job. We agreed to reconnect later.

And to put the icing on the cake, I am excited to share that Martina also completed her ICF Associate Certified Coach credential; she achieved everything that she set out to achieve and more through our coaching relationship. I was humbled and grateful that she chose me to help her achieve her dream career role.

STRATEGIES YOU LEARN FROM A COACH

In Chapter One, I addressed some of the issues that hold leaders back from being intentional leaders. Paraphrasing, I'm reminded of a line from Shakespeare—"heavy is the head that wears the crown." The challenges and sacrifices leaders confront come at a cost. Intentional leadership is no small quest to conquer, especially alone. Yet, the investment you make in working with a coach to become a more intentional leader serves as a gateway to developing your legacy as a leader that will live on beyond you.

In this section, I'm focusing on how a coach can be of value to you as a leader. Because it's critical that you know how to avoid what can hold leaders back, let's look at ways you might address them, especially if you recognize them as impeding your leadership.

These strategies are offered from the perspective of having coached hundreds of leaders over the years and supporting them in creating more positive and productive work environments in-person or virtually. These strategies are here to assist you in building stronger and healthier teams and organizations poised for greater success.

STRATEGIES FOR EFFECTIVE COMMUNICATION

Active Listening Skills

A coach can work with you as a leader to improve your active listening skills, teaching you how to fully focus on what others are saying by asking clarifying questions and validating the speaker's perspective. These two enhanced listening abilities contribute to more effective and empathetic communication.

Clarity and Conciseness

A coach can provide guidance to you on crafting clear and concise messages, helping you to eliminate unnecessary jargon and get to the point. This can ensure that your communication aligns with your audience's level of understanding whether it's one person or thousands. Clarity reduces misunderstandings and fosters better engagement.

Feedback Mechanisms

Coaches are available to assist you in establishing robust feedback mechanisms. As a leader, when you're able to actively seek input and get honest feedback, it's because you've been able to create an environment where team members feel comfortable providing it. Open, honest, and constructive feedback makes it possible for you to identify areas for improvement in your communication style.

Adaptability in Communication Styles

As a leader with a desire to be more inclusive in your communication, you might work with a coach to develop adaptability in your communication styles. Recognizing the diverse communication preferences within your team, your ability to adjust your approach requires an intention to engage more deeply. Intentional leaders are adept at switching between various communication styles to resonate with different team members. This is where you, as a leader, can lean into your awareness of strengths (as was addressed in the first part of the book, Pillar 1—Strengths Awareness).

STRATEGIES FOR RESISTANCE TO CHANGE

Change Management Leadership Skills

Leadership coaches work with you to develop skills specific to leading through change. In today's VUCA (volatility, uncertainties, complexities, and ambiguities) environment, given the elusiveness of change, it demands the support of a knowledgeable and trusted coach to guide you. That guidance includes understanding the psychology of change, effectively communicating the need for change, and creating a positive and supportive environment for your team and organization during transitional phases.

Building a Change-Ready Culture

Coaches work with leaders to foster a culture that embraces change. This involves promoting openness to new ideas, encouraging innovation, and recognizing and rewarding adaptability. As the leader, you set the example by being proactive in embracing change yourself.

Stakeholder Engagement

Leaders can learn strategies for engaging stakeholders in the change process. Coaches may guide you on effectively involving team members in decision-making, addressing concerns, and communicating the benefits of the proposed changes. When you engage stakeholders, it builds a sense of ownership and reduces resistance.

Resilience and Coping Mechanisms

Coaches assist leaders in developing personal resilience and coping mechanisms to deal with resistance. This includes stress management techniques, emotional intelligence development, and strategies for maintaining a positive outlook during challenging times. In the second part of the book, Pillar 2, you will find resources on building your resilience.

STRATEGIES FOR CONFLICT MANAGEMENT

Conflict Resolution Strategies

Coaches are equipped to teach leaders various conflict resolution strategies, emphasizing the importance of promptly and constructively addressing conflicts. This may involve mediation skills, negotiation techniques, and fostering a collaborative problem-solving mindset.

Emotional Intelligence

Leaders may focus on enhancing their emotional intelligence to better navigate conflicts. Coaches can be a bridge for leaders to understand their own emotions and those of others.

This helps you foster empathy and create an environment that's more conducive to resolving disputes.

Team Building Activities

Your coach might recommend team-building activities to strengthen relationships within your team. When you build a sense of camaraderie and mutual understanding, it can contribute to a more harmonious work environment. This, in all likelihood, will reduce conflicts.

Communication Training

Your coach can work with you on improving your communication skills and emphasizing clarity and transparency. When your communication is clear, it helps prevent misunderstandings that can escalate into conflicts. Be proactive and address potential issues before they escalate.

STRATEGIES FOR BALANCING RESPONSIBILITIES

Prioritization Techniques

A leadership coach guides you in developing intentional prioritization techniques. It involves brainstorming with you to identify and focus on high-impact tasks, appropriately delegate responsibilities, and maintain a balance between short-term and long-term goals.

Time Management Skills

A leader may work with a coach to enhance their time management skills. Some of what this addresses is your ability to set realistic goals, create schedules that allow for flexibility, and learn to say "no" when needed. "No" really is a complete sentence. If you want to say more, add "thank you." Improved time management contributes to reduced stress and better overall performance.

Delegation Strategies

Executive coaches can assist you in refining your delegation skills. Once again, this involves you understanding the strengths of your team members. It helps you assign tasks based on the individual's capabilities and provide the necessary support and resources. Intentional delegation empowers team members and allows them to focus on higher level strategic responsibilities.

Work-Life Well-Being Integration

Your executive coach may work with you to achieve a healthy and holistic work-life well-being integration. This holistic approach involves setting boundaries and promoting a culture that values work-life well-being integration that encourages you to prioritize self-care. Health care is the greatest wealth we have as individuals, and it begins with your personal self-care. An integrated intentional leader is more likely to be focused, energized, and capable of making sound decisions.

In each of these areas, an executive leadership coach plays a pivotal role in supporting your personal and professional development. Ultimately, it's about you becoming a more focused and intentional leader. My goal is to empower you with the skills and mindset needed to navigate challenges and lead your team to success on purpose and intentionally!

CHOOSING THE RIGHT COACH FOR YOU

The value of coaching is best achieved when you go all in for what you want. Clarity on what you hope to achieve through coaching is an important first step. Make time to research the background of the type of coach you want, then reach out to explore if they're the right coach for you.

Interview them to get a sense of energy between you. Compatibility matters when you're looking to work with a professional coach to help you transform your reality. Ask about their training, coaching experience, and credentials. Check them out on social media. Do they present themselves in ways that are acceptable to you? This is valuable information if you have an employer willing to invest in your leadership development and professional growth. Dr. Helen Holton and Associates has an Intentional Leadership Process System™ with proven results that drive leaders like you forward to your what's next.

You want your leadership development program to have a credentialed, professional coach who continually invests in their own leadership development and professional growth. The better leaders they become, the greater the benefit they bring to you and those you lead. Your coach wants nothing less than your best to help you become all you are meant to be.

A coach doesn't have the answers for you in a coaching relationship. As your consultant, they can offer you solutions, however, this is a different type of engagement that is outside the realm of coaching. The value of coaching increases when you have a professionally trained and credentialed coach who is held accountable by a global professional organization like the International Coaching Federation (ICF).

ICF is the world's most highly regarded organization that provides credentialing to coaches who have been vetted, tested, and adhere to ICF's set of ethical guidelines to attain their credentials. For more information on ICF, visit www.coachingfederation.org. It is through continuous professional development, adherence to ethical guidelines, and accountability measures in place that allow a coach to hold themselves out to the public with distinction.

REFLECTION QUESTIONS AND NOTES

Who holds you accountable to achieve your hopes and dreams as a leader?

How can a coaching relationship help you navigate challenges and complex decisions as a leader?

Make a list of how feedback, insights, and a safe space with a professional coach can enhance your leadership.

AN INVITATION TO SHIFT FORWARD INTO INTENTIONAL LEADERSHIP

For me, the purpose has always been to remain in pursuit of achievement with excellence and to maintain the ability to rebound when knocked down. The mission remains the same throughout my multiple sectors of service. The goal is clear—to keep rising forward and doing good by guiding leaders to become better leaders, more intentional leaders by design and on purpose. The diversity of my background, experiences, and earned expertise across various industries and sectors has shaped my leadership to be broad and deep at the same time.

I've taken risks and stepped into the unknown more times than I can remember. There have been times when I wasn't sure of what I was stepping into, and I stepped into them anyway. Some were calculated, and others were stupid. I've won more than I lost and learned from them all. One of the biggest learnings was how to fail forward.

Focusing on the past and lamenting your failures are not worth your time or effort to dwell on what could have been if…. That's a path you don't want to go down and get stuck in yesterday because it'll rob you of your present moment. You'll miss the life you're living now and the opportunities all around you to make life better, especially as a leader. Don't get me wrong—reflecting and looking behind you is a powerful tool to propel you forward, to grow. It's a good thing to do.

Make sure you're reflecting for the right reasons. You are the architect of your life. Be clear that what you're reflecting on is leading you forward and not pulling you backwards into what's already done and can't be changed. Spilled milk is spilled milk. You can't put it back in the container. Clean up the mess as best you can and move forward.

Yes, I know, that's easier said than done. However, it will save you time and resources in getting to where you want to be—forward looking, thinking, thriving, and living. Getting to the place of writing this book is nothing short of kicking procrastination in the butt and moving it out of my way—boldly looking fear in the face and pressing forward.

I've learned a lot and realized that sharing the challenges, missteps, successes, and just plain dumb stuff I've done might benefit you or someone you know who's stuck and wants to move forward. Every valuable lesson doesn't have to be learned by experience. Learning from the mistakes of others can save you time, money, and self-blame or shame.

So, where do you go from here now that you've come to the end of the book? At Dr. Helen Holton and Associates, we understand the challenges leaders like yourself face in today's dynamic business landscape. We have developed an innovative and integrated program designed to catalyze intentional shifts in leadership. It propels leaders, teams, and organizations toward unparalleled success.

Our cutting-edge Intentional Leadership Process System™ goes beyond conventional leadership models, aimed to empower leaders in how to navigate complexities, drive positive change, and foster a culture of continuous improvement. We firmly believe that by implementing intentional shifts in leadership, you can unlock your full potential and achieve sustained excellence as a leader.

This is your invitation to explore what's next. To provide you with more insight into the possibilities that lie ahead, I invite you to schedule a brief, no-obligation conversation with me. It will be an opportunity for us to understand your organization's unique needs and how our program can be tailored to drive the intentional shift in leadership you aspire to achieve. Visit **drhelenholton.com** to get started.

We look forward to collaborating with you to elevate your leadership and the success of your team to the level of achieving intentional leadership throughout your organization.

ABOUT THE AUTHOR

Helen Holton is an accomplished, tried, and true intentional leader who is a contributing author of several books, best-selling and award winners. After thirty years as an elected official and executive director of a national nonprofit for county officials, she knows something about leadership. As the founder and CEO of Dr. Helen Holton and Associates, a boutique firm that partners with leaders to drive their visions and teams forward, she reimagined life. Today, Dr. Helen lives out her passion, purpose, and calling as an executive and leadership coach, trainer, facilitator, consultant, speaker, and author.

Dr. Holton holds several credentials and is a certified practitioner of the following:

- Certified Personal and Executive Coach (CPEC)
- Certified Professional Co-Active Coach (CPCC)
- Certified Virtual Master Presenter (VMP)

- Gallup-Certified Strengths Coach and Trainer
- Hogan Leadership Assessment Certified and 360 Profile Administrator
- Intercultural Development Inventory® (IDI) Qualified Administrator
- The Maxwell DISC Method Certified Consultant
- Mentor Coach with ICF
- PCC (Professional Certified Coach) with International Coaching Federation (ICF)
- Society of Human Resources-Certified Professional (SHRM-CP)
- Team Coaching Foundations Certified Coach

Dr. Helen brings authentic truths, beliefs, and perspectives to engagements without personal attachment. She shares from a sincere space of curiosity and caring with the intention to evoke a deeper level of engagement, transparency, and honesty to the work you do as a leader. Your investment in human capital to build and strengthen a more Inclusive, Resilient and Respectful (IRR) environment leads to a genuine sense of belonging for all and a stronger ROI or return on investment.

IRR also stands for Internal Rate of Return and refers to a method of calculating an investment's rate of return that excludes external factors such as the risk-free rate, inflation, the cost of capital, or financial risk. (Remember, I'm a licensed CPA, and we keep a focus on the bottom line!) To be IRR—that is, Inclusive, Resilient, and Respectful—is to have a posture of intent exercised by an intentional leader who is focused on the bottom line of financial performance and on how to drive their team and organization to achieve success. The two are related. IRR in finances is best achieved when leaders show up as Inclusive, Resilient, and Respectful people toward everyone they encounter and serve.

When Dr. Helen is not in pursuit of her purpose, passion, and calling, you can find her traveling to experience new lands, exotic spa treatments, indulging in food adventures, attempting to play better golf, and socializing with friends and family, near and far.

ABOUT DR. HELEN HOLTON AND ASSOCIATES

Who are you at your best? The journey begins with self-awareness. Dr. Helen Holton and Associates partners with you to enhance awareness of your strengths; visualize viable opportunities; gain valuable insights; and accomplish meaningful visions, goals, and dreams in times of substantial organizational shifts and unpredictability. Leaders report outcomes of greater clarity, better communication, and deeper engagement in their organizations, leading to stronger bottom-line results. The list of leaders and teams successfully practicing intentional leadership through her program continues to grow.

After examining years of research from listening to leaders, it was clear for Dr. Helen Holton that a safe space and trusted place were needed to confront challenges, fears, and procrastination to get unstuck and move forward. The outcome led to the creation of Dr. Helen's Intentional Leadership

Process System™, a multi-faceted solution to break down barriers and build bridges to achieve better outcomes. She's the outsider who comes into your organization without judgment or preconceived perspectives.

Connect and stay in touch with Dr. Helen Holton and Associates at drhelenholton.com and @DrHelenHolton on LinkedIn, Instagram, Twitter, Facebook, and YouTube.

RESOURCES

Blanchard, Ken and Phil Hodges, *Lead Like Jesus: Lessons for Everyone from the Greatest Leadership Role Model of All Time.* (Nashville: W Pub Group, a part of Thomas Nelson, 2006).

Buckingham, Marcus, *Love and Work: How to Find What You Love, Love What You Do, and Do It for the Rest of Your Life.* (Brighton, MA: Harvard Business Review Press, 2022).

Cameron, Kim, *Practicing Positive Leadership: Tools and Techniques That Create Extraordinary Results.* (Oakland: Berrett-Koehler Publishers, 2013).

Clifton, Jim and Jim Harter, *Culture Shock: An unstoppable force is changing how we work and live. Gallup's solution to the biggest leadership issue of our time.* (Washington, DC: Gallup Press, 2023).

———, *Wellbeing at Work: How to Build Resilient and Thriving Teams.* (Washington, DC: Gallup Press, 2021).

Clifton, Jim and Sangeeta Bharadwaj Badal, PhD, *Entrepreneurial StrengthsFinder.* (Washington, DC: Gallup Press, 2014).

———, *Born to Build: How to Build a Thriving Startup, a Winning Team, New Customers and Your Best Life Imaginable.* (Washington, DC: Gallup Press, 2018).

Clifton, Jon, *Blind Spot: The Global Rise of Unhappiness and How Leaders Missed It.* (Washington, DC: Gallup Press, 2022).

Covey, Stephen R. and Sean Covey, *The 7 Habits of Highly Effective People: 30th Anniversary Card Deck (The Official 7 Habits Card Deck).* (Salt Lake City: FranklinCovey, 2019).

Fickett, Lloyd and Jason Fickett, *The Collaborative Way: A Story About Engaging the Mind and Spirit of a Company.* (Independently published, 2006).

Goleman, Daniel, Richard E. Boyatzis, and Annie McKee, *Primal Leadership: Unleashing the Power of Emotional Intelligence.* (Brighton, MA: Harvard Business Review Press, 2013).

Gordon, Jon, *The Energy Bus: 10 Rules to Fuel Your Work, Life, and Team with Positive Energy.* (Hoboken, NJ: Wiley, 2007).

———, *The Power of Positive Leadership: How and Why Positive Leaders Transform Teams and Organizations and Change the World.* (Hoboken, NJ: Wiley, 2017).

Harris, Carla, *Lead to Win: How to Be a Powerful, Impactful, Influential Leader in Any Environment.* (New York: Avery, an imprint of Random House, 2022).

Hermann, Ned and Ann Hermann-Nehdi, *The Whole Brain Business Book: Unlocking the Power of Whole Brain Thinking in Organizations, Teams, and Individuals.* (New York: McGraw-Hill, 2015).

Kouzes, James M. and Barry Z. Posner, *The Leadership Challenge: How to Make Extraordinary Things Happen in Organizations.* (Hoboken, NJ: Wiley, 2017).

Lencioni, Patrick, *The Five Dysfunctions of a Team: A Leadership Fable.* (Hoboken, NJ: Jossey-Bass, 2011).

Maxwell, John C., *The 16 Undeniable Laws of Communication: Apply Them and Make the Most of Your Message.* (Duluth, GA: Maxwell Leadership, 2023).

———, *The 21 Indispensable Qualities of a Leader: Becoming the Person Others Will Want to Follow*, 2nd ed. (Nashville: HarperCollins Leadership, 2007).

———, *Developing the Leader Within You 2.0.* (Nashville: HarperCollins Leadership, 2018).

———, *Everyone Communicates Few Connect: What the Most Effective People Do Differently.* (Nashville: HarperCollins Leadership, 2010).

———, *The Greatest Story Ever Told*, lead ed. (New York: Center Street, 2016).

———, *The 21 Irrefutable Laws of Leadership: Follow Them and People Will Follow You*, twenty-fifth anniversary ed. (Nashville: HarperCollins Leadership, 2022).

———, *Intentional Living: Choosing a Life that Matters*, reprint ed. (New York: Center Street, 2017).

———, *The Leader's Greatest Return: Attracting, Developing, and Multiplying Leaders.* (Nashville: HarperCollins Leadership, 2020).

Maxwell, John C. and Rob Hoskins, *Change Your World: How Anyone, Anywhere Can Make a Difference.* (Nashville: HarperCollins Leadership, 2021).

Rath, Tom and Barry Conchie, *Strengths Based Leadership: Great Leaders, Teams, and Why People Follow.* (Washington, DC: Gallup Press, 2008).

Rock, David and Linda J. Page, PhD, *Coaching with the Brain in Mind: Foundations for Practice.* (Hoboken, NJ: Wiley, 2009).

Senge, Peter M., *The Fifth Discipline: The Art and Practice of the Learning Organization*, revised ed. (New York: Doubleday, 2006).

Winseman, Albert L., Donald O. Clifton, PhD, and Curt Liesveld, MDiv, MA., *Living Your Strengths: Discover Your God-Given Talents and Inspire Your Community*, 2nd ed. (Washington, DC: Gallup Press, 2004).

NOTES

Pillar 1

1. Jim Clifton, "Build Your Career Around Your Strengths, Not Your Weaknesses." Gallup website, October 5, 2022, accessed April 8, 2024, https://www.gallup.com/workplace/402500/build-career-around-strengths-not-weaknesses.aspx.

Chapter 5

1. "CliftonStrengths (Formerly StrengthsFinder) Research and Where It All Began." Gallup website, accessed April 8, 2024, https://www.gallup.com/cliftonstrengths/en/253790/science-of-cliftonstrengths.aspx.
2. "Donald Clifton, 79; Former Head of Gallup Polling Firm." *Los Angeles Times* website, September 19, 2003, accessed April 8, 2024, https://www.latimes.com/archives/la-xpm-2003-sep-19-me-passings19.3-story.html.

Chapter 6

1. "How to Improve Your Career Development." Gallup website, accessed April 8, 2024, https://www.gallup.com/cliftonstrengths/en/299855/how-to-improve-my-career.aspx#:~:text=Answering%20the%20%22What%20Are%20Your,than%20just%20the%20interview%20process.

2. "What is the Definition of Discipline?" Gallup website, accessed July 27, 2024, https://www.gallup.com/cliftonstrengths/en/252227/discipline-theme.aspx#:~:text=People%20exceptionally%20talented%20in%20the,Discipline%2C%20are%20strongest%20in%20them.

Chapter 9

1. "Struggle," Dictionary.com website, accessed April 1, 2024, https://www.dictionary.com/browse/struggle#google_vignette.

Chapter 11

1. "Wellness," Dictionary.com website, accessed April 8, 2024, https://www.dictionary.com/browse/wellness.

2. "Well-being," Dictionary.com website, accessed April 8, 2024, https://www.dictionary.com/browse/well-being.

Chapter 12

1. Melissa Madeson, PhD, "Seligman's PERMA+ Model Explained: A Theory of Wellbeing." Positive Psychology website, February 24, 2017, accessed April 8, 2024, https://positivepsychology.com/perma-model/.

2. "Mihaly Csikszentmihalyi: The Father of Flow." Claremont Graduate University website, accessed April 8, 2024, https://www.cgu.edu/people/mihaly-csikszentmihalyi/.

3. Ibid.

4. "Mihaly Csikszentmihalyi & Flow," Pursuit of Happiness website, accessed April 8, 2024, https://www.pursuit-of-happiness.org/history-of-happiness/mihaly-csikszentmihalyi/#:~:text=Cziksentmihalyi%20defines%20flow%20as%20%E2%80%9Ca,(Cskikszentmihalyi%2C%20 1990%2C%20p.

5. Peter Flade, Jim Asplund, and Gwen Elliot, "Employees Who Use Their Strengths Outperform Those Who Don't." Gallup website. October 8, 2015, accessed July 28, 2024, https://www.gallup.com/workplace/236561/employees-strengths-outperform-don.aspx.

6. Anthony M. Grant, "ROI is a Poor Measure of Coaching Success: Towards a More Holistic Approach Using a Well-being and Engagement Framework." *Coaching: An International Journal of Theory, Research and Practice*, 5, no. 2 (September 2012): 1–12. http://dx.doi.org/10.1080/17521882.2012.672438.

7. Ibid.

8. Ibid.

www.ingramcontent.com/pod-product-compliance
Lightning Source LLC
Chambersburg PA
CBHW030910060726
47591CB00005B/1481